EXPLORING HERE & THERE

GLEANINGS OVER MANY YEARS

100 Sermon Starters & Devotional Studies

VOLUME II

JOHN PHILLIPS

AMBASSADOR-EMERALD INTERNATIONAL
GREENVILLE, SOUTH CAROLINA • BELFAST, NORTHERN IRELAND

Published by:
Ambassador-Emerald International
427 Wade Hampton Blvd.
Greenville, SC 29609 USA

and

Ambassador Productions
Ardenlee Street
Belfast, BT6 8QJ
Northern Ireland

www.emeraldhouse.com

Cover and internal design by Matt Donovan
Cover design © 2000 Grand Design

DEDICATION

I dedicate this book to Betty for whom these devotional studies were written.

When I was courting her Betty lived in California and I lived in North Carolina. Three thousand miles and three time zones stretched between. As a result, much of our courting was done on the telephone. In time I ran out of things to say!

I decided to write her a devotional every day. By the time I was finished I had written nearly three hundred of them.

Here they are, with her earnest desire that they might be as great a blessing to you as they have been to her.

John Phillips

CONTENTS

"I Have Commanded The Ravens"
1 Kings 17:1-7

The great prophet, Elijah, had burst like a tornado into the presence of Ahab and Jezebel. He had with him a key that could lock or unlock the sun, the rain, the wind and the storm. Before the astonished eyes of that godless and guilty King and Queen, Elijah locked up the rain. "No more rain!" he said, "No more rain but according to my word." Then he stormed back out of the royal presence and vanished from view. And he remained hidden for three and a half years while great tribulation fell on the land. "Go hide thyself," God said. Later He would say: "Go show thyself." God invariably conceals his man before He reveals His man.

During this three and a half year period, Elijah was hidden by God in a wadi and then by a widow. By the <u>winding brook</u>, Elijah developed a faith that could conquer drought. By the <u>wasting barrel</u>, in the widow's bare kitchen, Elijah developed a hope that could conquer despair. By that <u>widow's boy</u>, Elijah developed a faith that could conquer death. Once he had learned these lessons, God was able to use him as few have ever been used before or since. Israel's faith was as <u>dry</u> as that brook. Israel's hope was as <u>dismal</u> as that depleted barrel, and Israel's love was as <u>dead</u> as that boy. Elijah, having learned <u>personally</u> how to deal with such things, could now deal with them publicly.

But let us spend some time with the great prophet as he sits beside that drying brook in a hidden place, far from the haunts and habitations of men. And let us recall the Lord's own words to His own about the raven: "Consider" He said, "Consider the ravens" (Lk. 12:24-28). Elijah certainly must have considered them during those days beside that brook. He looked forward to their visits twice a day.

There was, for instance, their COLOR, black and glossy. Elijah would doubtless think of the Shulamite, in Solomon's spirit-born song, and her description of her beloved: "His locks," she said, "are bushy and black as the raven" (5:11). That reminder would take Elijah's soul by storm, for the Shulamite's words reached far beyond her own beloved. They pointed to Another, One Who was yet to come, One to Whom the Shulamite's Beloved

1

was but a type. Elijah's thoughts took wing. From the visiting ravens and from the shepherd-love of the Shulamite, his thoughts would soar down the centuries from the Shulamite's beloved to Heaven's Beloved. So, the color of the ravens alone reminded the lonely prophet of Christ.

Then he considered their CRY. As they dropped their tribute at his feet and wheeled away into the setting sun, Elijah would think, perhaps, of the Psalmist's words, "Sing unto the Lord with thanksgiving. . . . He giveth to the beast his prey and to the young ravens which cry" (Ps. 147:9). True, the ravens waited on his table in the wilds; but it was God Himself Who spread the feast.

Moreover he would consider their CHARACTER. The Levitical law would come to his mind. Moses had specifically pronounced ravens to be unclean: "And these are they which ye shall have in abomination among the fowls . . . every raven after his kind (Lev.11:15). The raven by nature was an unclean bird.

The black, unclean birds would remind Elijah of the abomination that rode triumphant in Israel, spurred on by Jezebel and urged on by hundreds of her attendant court-priests. He would take courage as he viewed the ravens coming from afar.

If God could so cleanse ravens, and make them ministers to His own, then there was nothing too hard for God. He had changed the very nature of these birds so that twice a day they brought him beef and bread to eat. He could change the heart of erring Israel.

Finally, the prophet would consider their COURSE, as he watched them whirling and diving in the sky. He would remember the first mention of crows in the Bible. God have given them room in the ark; but, at the first opportunity, they went back to their wild, corrupt and carnal ways. Unlike the dove, which came eagerly back to the ark from its flight abroad, the crows preferred a world where death reigned.

So, sitting by his brook, Elijah drew lessons from the ravens; and his faith grew strong. There was nothing too hard for God. The man who had thus learned to look to heaven for FOOD would soon be able to look to heaven for his FIRE.

AN ALMOST EMPTY BARREL
1 KINGS 17:1-7

The barrel belonged to a widow. She was not even a Hebrew widow. The law of Moses made provision for Hebrew widows and orphans, but this woman had no such resource. Her case was desperate. All that remained to her, all that stood between her and starvation in a cold, pitiless world was an almost empty barrel. Almost empty but not quite.

The prophet Elijah had been sent to meet this widow. He had been staying by a brook but it had run dry and God had directed him to go to Zarephath, an outpost of Zidon where he would be cared for by a widow. Elijah's reactions were probably mixed. "A widow?" he might have exclaimed. I wonder if she is young or old, good-looking or plain? rich or poor? But Zidon! Why that is where Jezebel comes from. Her father, Eth-baal, is King of the Zidonians; and that could be dangerous for me. Jezebel is scouring the land to lay her hands on me. But Elijah, however, had not become a prince of prophets by running away from danger. So, off he went to find his widow. Centuries later Jesus reminded his neighbors at Nazareth that there were many widows in Israel in the days of Elijah, but God did not send Elijah to any of them. He sent him to a Gentile widow. Thus Elijah became the first prophet to the Gentiles.

We can picture their first encounter. The widow he met, at last, was evidently poor, and she had a child tied to her apron strings. Probably the prophet was far from impressed. "Excuse me, ma'am," he might have said, "do you know of any rich widows around here? I am a prophet. God has told me I will find a widow from these parts who will give me room and board."

"I'm that widow."

"Is that so? Well, please bring me some water and I am hungry so please bring me something to eat."

"All I have is a handful of meal in a barrel, just enough for me and my son. I am going home to make a small biscuit. I shall share it with my son and then we shall starve to death."

A handful of meal! That was all. Of course, it all depends on whose hand is full. It so happened, in this case, that the hand that was full was the hand of God, the hand that holds the prairies. That hand could never fail.

There are three factors in the equation of this interlude in Elijah's ministry. First, there was handful of <u>meal</u> in her near-empty barrel. That meal spoke of the Christ. The second great offering of the Mosaic law was the <u>meal</u> offering. It pictured the sinless humanity of the Lord Jesus, pure, even, crushed beneath the millstones and fit to be offered to God.

But this widow had something else, something that almost gets overlooked. She had "a little <u>oil</u> in her flask." That oil would blend with the meal and make the dough for a small cake. It speaks of the Holy Spirit. The Holy Spirit is part of everything Jesus said, and did, and was. He was conceived of the Holy Spirit, filled with the Holy Spirit, anointed by the Holy Spirit and offered in sacrifice to God through the Holy Spirit. As the flour and the oil were blended together so the Son and the Spirit were blended together.

There was one other factor in this Old Testament equation of Christ. The woman was holding <u>two sticks</u>. The two sticks, surely, represent the <u>cross</u>. It takes two sticks to make a cross, no more, no less. The woman had a firm grip on needed, <u>Christ</u>, the Christ of the meal offering; the <u>Comforter</u>, the oil in a vessel; and the <u>Cross</u>. They saw her through to the end.

That nearly empty barrel was never quite empty, that oil was just enough for each and every day, and Calvary took care of it all. God does not ask much of us when we first come into contact with Him in our deep need. But He does insist that we have some grasp on the Christ, the Comforter and the Cross. That will see us through.

A DEAD BOY

1 KINGS 17:17-24

The long and the short of it was that the boy was dead. His mother had a dead son on her hands, and she knew it. Many people have the same problem. They have children who are very much alive to all that this world has to offer, but who are, just the same, spiritual dead, "dead in trespasses and sins." This mother had done all that a mother could do for her son, but now he was beyond all human help. She turned to the one man she knew who knew a God she did not know.

There are three people in the story, the dead boy, the distraught mother and the distressed prophet. The problem with the boy was physical, the problem of the woman was emotional, the problem of the prophet was spiritual. The child cried to his mother, the mother cried to the prophet and the prophet cried to God. The tragedy, in that little cottage in that pagan town, gives us a glimpse of why God allows sorrow to come into our lives. With the widow, for instance, it led to confession. With Elijah it led to compassion.

With the woman it led to CONFESSION OF SIN. We are not told what her sin was. Likely enough, it had something to do with idolatry. She was a pagan, but a pagan to whom God had spoken. The idolatry of the Canaanites involved the grossest immorality. Few could have escaped it. Perhaps the woman had once been engaged in some aspect of the immorality of her religion. Perhaps her boy was its fruit. In time, the woman had come to idolize her child. When Elijah had asked for a piece of bread, she told him that all she had was a handful of meal. "It is just enough for one small meal for <u>me</u> and <u>my son</u>," she said. Before it was all over, the prophet would say: in the name of the living God "Give <u>me</u> thy son." That is about all we can do with spiritually dead children, give them to God, totally and without reservation.

Gazing at her dead child a sense of her sin suddenly overwhelmed this woman: "What have I to do with thee, O thou man of God?" she cried, "have you come to bring my sin to remembrance and to slay my son?" It suddenly dawned on her that she was a sinner, though Elijah had said nothing at all about sin. The mere presence of a truly holy person often has that effect on guilty people.

We turn now to the prophet himself. In all this, God wanted to develop within the prophet a COMPASSION OF SOUL. Elijah was the prophet of the Law and not overly famous for his grace. There was a great deal of difference, for example, between Moses and Elijah. Moses, who unveiled the Law and Elijah, who upheld the Law. Moses interceded for <u>Israel</u>, but Elijah interceded <u>against</u> Israel. Both men were prophets; but whereas Moses was essentially a thoughtful pastor, Elijah was essentially a thundering preacher. Moses brought down food from heaven, Elijah brought down fire.

The death of the widow's boy touched the very heart of the prophet. Doubtless he had grown fond of the boy. "Give me thy son," he said in response to the widow's cry. He gathered the dead boy up in his arms (we never read of him doing that before), and carried the corpse up the stairs to his room. He placed it on his bed. Then he prayed.

His prayer consisted of just twenty words, that was all. It can be said in five seconds. Truly we are not heard for our much speaking. Prayer is not measured by its length but by its depth.

Then Elijah stretched himself upon the corpse. By so doing, he stood before God as a man defiled, for the Mosaic law pronounced all who touched a dead body to be unclean. By this act the prophet, in effect, said to God: "O God, this boy is dead, and the <u>law</u> can do nothing for him. The law cannot minister life. I therefore disqualify myself, as a man of the Law, from being able to do anything at all for this boy. If anything is to be done for this dead boy, then something above and beyond the "law" must take over. So I put this matter before you, not on the basis of Law, but on the basis of grace." No wonder, within minutes, he was able to say to the widow: "See, thy son liveth."

That is what we must do for our dead sons and daughters. We cannot legislate holiness or command our children to be good. Even the Law of God itself cannot impart life. But grace can, and does. Blessed be God!

OBADIAH OF SAMARIA
1 KINGS 18:1-16

It is Obadiah's lasting misfortune that when we take his measure, he is not standing alone, by himself. Otherwise we might have thought him a giant. But, unfortunately for Obadiah he is always standing alongside Elijah, a giant indeed. Elijah not only made poor Obadiah look like a pygmy, he treated him with scant respect. But we are letting our story run away with us.

Let us begin with Obadiah's TESTIMONY. The Holy Spirit says that "Obadiah feared the Lord greatly." Just the same, Obadiah was afraid of King Ahab and even more afraid of Jezebel. The two of them were a formidable pair. Jezebel was determined to stamp out the worship of Jehovah in Israel and had imported over eight hundred pagan priests and prophets to accomplish her end. Obadiah was more afraid of her then he was of God. Small wonder. Even Elijah ran away from her.

Obadiah was an official at Ahab's court. He ran the royal household. He knew how matters stood. He was afraid of Ahab. Ahab was afraid of Jezebel. Jezebel was afraid of nobody.

Though Obadiah's fear of God was flawed, nevertheless the Holy Spirit bears this witness to pose Obadiah that "Obadiah feared the Lord greatly."

There were one hundred Hebrew prophets in Israel who Jezebel wanted put to death and it was a criminal offense to help them. They had gone into hiding, and Jezebel's secret police scoured the country looking for them. There was one man who knew where they were—Obadiah. He had hidden them. Moreover he took advantage of his position as Ahab's steward to smuggle food and drink to them. God honored him for that. Such as his testimony. He had faith. But he lived with fear as well.

Next, we have Obadiah's TASK. He was ordered by Ahab to search the whole country in the hope of finding enough grass to feed the royal horses and mules—a well-nigh hopeless task. The drought Elijah had imposed on Israel had lasted now for three and a half years and the land was bare. Obadiah did not have the courage to point out to Ahab that it was his apostasy that was responsible for the state of affairs in Israel. He went off on his hopeless errand.

And then he met Elijah. He could hardly believe his eyes. There was an enormous price on Elijah's head. He was the object of a massive nationwide man hunt. "Go and tell Ahab I'm here," he said. Which brings us to Obadiah's TERROR. "Why!" he said, "Ahab's police are looking for you everywhere. Ahab's ambassadors have agreements with all the surrounding countries to extradite you should you surface in one of them. This is a trick. I'll go and get the King, and the moment my back is turned the Spirit of God will whisk you away and I'll be left to face the fury of Ahab and Jezebel. What have I sinned that you want to betray me like that? Is this my reward for hiding those prophets?"

Well, Obadiah had his day in the spotlight. Elijah lived in it. "Obadiah," we read, "went to meet Ahab." And that is the last we hear of him. "Obadiah went to meet Ahab." Then we read: "And Ahab went to meet Elijah." There lies the difference. Obadiah was ruled by caution; Elijah was ruled by conviction. Obadiah was one of those seven thousand the Lord talked about, men who had now bowed the knee to Baal. That's the best we can say about him. Elijah took heaven by storm. Obadiah limped along the highway home. Still, God gives him credit where credit is due. He "feared the Lord greatly." Far more than most of his countrymen did. God writes it into His Book. What does He write into His Book about us?

THE GOD THAT ANSWERETH BY FIRE

1 KINGS 18:24

Elijah was unique among the prophets. Obadiah was supporting no less than one hundred of them; but, one and all, they cowered in a cave in fear for their lives. Much good they were doing! Not so Elijah. He was made of sterner stuff. He was a veritable Mechizedek among the prophets, presented, as it were, "without father or mother, without beginning or ending of days, a prophet of the Most High God."

Summoned into his presence, the weak and wicked king Ahab tried bluster and bravado. Elijah shut him up. "Get your priests and people to Carmel," He demanded. "We'll put things to the test." And, for the moment, more afraid of Elijah than of Jezebel, Ahab agreed. After all, Ahab thought, what could one lone man do against 450 priests and prophets of Baal? Not much!

We look first at THE CULT. The ministers of its foul and fierce rituals were an unholy crew. The hideous and polluted apostasy they championed, had it won the battle on Mount Carmel that day, would have obliterated the name and memory of Israel from the roll call of the nations. The terms of the contest were simple. The 450 prophets of Baal were to be given a bullock. And Elijah was to have one, too. Each in turn would sacrifice their animal and place it on the altar. Then the god that answered by fire would acknowledged to be God. In growing despair, the false prophets of Baal worked themselves into a frenzy. Elijah stood by and mocked them with a fine flow of sarcasm. There lay their dead bullock on its bed of wood. There in the sky, long past its meridian, their Zidonian sun god was sinking into the sea Baal's prophets and priests cried aloud. They slashed themselves. They worked themselves into a frenzy. All in vain. The sun continued to sink unmoved by it all.

Now let us look at THE CROWD. All day long they had watched the antics of the Baal cult. Now it was Elijah's turn. Calmly he repaired an old mountain altar. Then deliberately he slew his bullock. He placed it on the altar. Around the altar he dug a wide trench. Then he had twelve barrels of water poured all over the altar and filled the trench as well.

The crowd gathered around as the evening shadows began to steal across the sky. Then Elijah prayed. The fire fell. It was a good thing for the people there that day that a sacrifice lay there upon the altar dressed and ready for the fire. "Our God is a consuming fire," the Bible says. And so He is. The flame descending from on high would have landed on the people and consumed them all had there been no altar there. Instead, it fell upon the sacrifice. In type and symbol Elijah put the cross between that holy God in heaven and that sinful people on earth. The only ones who died that day were the prophets of Baal, slain by Elijah for the wickedness they had wrought.

Then came THE CLOUD. The great tribulation was over! Elijah who had just appealed to heaven for <u>fire</u>, now appealed to heaven for <u>rain</u>. "He prayed," the Holy Spirit says. He and his servant divided the task. The servant was to watch; Elijah was to pray. And so he did, until a cloud like a man's hand appeared in the sky, until prophet's upraised hand left its imprint on the sky. Then down came the rain.

Obadiah's hidden prophets did not bring the rain that day. Elijah did. They could not have brought the fire either. God does not give the key of heaven and power over the forces of earth to such as they.

"WHAT DOEST THOU HERE ELIJAH?"

I KINGS 19:9, 13

"What does thou here Elijah?" The question is asked twice in less than half a dozen verses. And the prophet gives the same sad reply both times.

It is often helpful, in opening up a verse or so of Scripture, to go through the passage putting the emphasis on a different word each time— "What <u>doest</u> thou here Elijah?" Well, of course, he was doing nothing, just sitting at Sinai feeling sorry for himself. "What doest <u>thou</u> here Elijah?" He, of all people! The man who had just come from Carmel and a glorious, miraculous victory! "What does thou <u>here</u> Elijah?" Sitting in the shadow of Sinai, forty days journey from the sphere of duty, as though more edicts from the holy mount could help either him or his people. "What doest thou here <u>Elijah</u>?" His name is a combination of the two primary names for God—Elohim and Jehovah—The God of Creation, omnipotent in power; the God of Covenant, matchless in grace. What was a man with a name like that doing at Sinai when he should have been at Samaria?

Elijah, fearless before Ahab, had fled from Jezebel. Now the reaction had set in. The day after a great victory is always a time of danger for the child of God because Satan always counterattacks. Elijah, with Jezebel's threats curdling his blood, had fled a day's journey into the wilderness. He felt himself friendless and alone. Already the baying of the bloodhounds could be heard, sounding across the desert.

His flight appalled him. "I am no better than my fathers," he moaned. "Let me die!" he said. "Come and dine," God replied. God knew His man was exhausted physically and spiritually. "Let me die!" That was self-pity speaking. After all if Elijah had <u>really</u> wanted to die, all he needed to do was let Jezebel know where he was! In any case, God had something far better than martyrdom in store for Elijah.

So an angel came, cooked the prophet's supper for him, and then his breakfast. Restored physically, the prophet went in the strength of those two meals for forty days, all the way to Sinai. Now, far from where he should have been, Elijah had a fresh fit of the sulks. God challenged him:

"What doest thou here Elijah?" "I, even I, am the only one left," he moaned—something that was obviously not true. There was Obadiah and his hidden prophets to start with. They may not have been calling down fire but they had certainly not bowed the knee to Baal either.

God had revealed Himself as a <u>sympathizing</u> God. Now He reveals Himself as a <u>sufficient</u> God.

First we see the mount of God: "Go and stand upon the mount before the Lord," God said. Elijah's hero Moses had climbed that awesome peak of Sinai no less than seven times in receiving the Law. Now it was Elijah's turn. Up he went. And there he stood, hiding from a hurricane, from a terrifying earthquake and from a fearful, flaming fire. Each of these awesome exhibits of God's power passed before the shaken prophet, but God was no in any of them. They were tools God had at His disposal. He was just reminding His run-away prophet that He had all kinds of instruments with which to fight Jezebel, if He wanted to use them. So, why be afraid of Jezebel?

"Yes, Elijah," God said, "I can tear, but I much prefer to teach." So the forces of nature were all replaced by a still small voice. "Yes, my child, I can perform miracles. You ought to know that. I loaned you my weapon of fire on Carmel. But miracles are not all that effective. It is my WORD that produces the best results. The wind can blow, the fire can burn and the earthquake can break; but My Word, still and small to your mortal ears, is "quick and powerful and sharper than any two-edged sword" (Heb 4:12).

After all this, God asked the prophet again: What doest thou here Elijah?" "I'm the only one left. They want to kill me," said Elijah. Still full of self-pity the prophet repeated word-for-word what he had said before.

"That's enough!" God said. "Go and anoint Elisha to replace you." That's <u>one</u> you didn't know about whose knees have never bowed to Baal. And, by the way, I have seven thousand faithful saints who have not bowed to Baal. You don't know any of them. I know all of them."

But God is very kind. He did not answer Elijah's plea to die. Not a bit of it! He allowed him to train his successor. Then, blessed be God, He sent a chariot of fire and an angel escort to carry him straight into the Glory! How good and gracious a God He is.

A SUCCESSOR FOR ELIJAH

I KINGS 19:19

There were scores of men in Israel who would have jumped at a change to have been Elijah's successor. Obadiah had a caveful of them. The school of the prophets had some more of them. The Spirit of God, however, passed over all of them. He already had his man in mind, one Elisha, a man with no theological training or prophetic experience at all.

There are three things about Elisha. First, he was a SUCCESSFUL FARMER. When Elijah found him, he was at work. He had twelve yoke of oxen, harnessed to a plow and was driving straight furrows across the face of a field. Elijah's heart warmed to him at once. Here was a man who had learned how to follow a plow, how to put his hand to the plow and never look back, a man fit, by the Lord's own standard, to inherit the Kingdom of God. Elijah threw his mantle on him. Within the hour, Elisha had taken his plow and chopped it up for firewood. He had taken his two prize oxen and made a burnt offering of them. He had called a hasty "goodbye" to his family and had run as fast as he could to catch up with the Master. He never looked back.

Now we look at the SUBMISSIVE DISCIPLE. He learned many things from the master while running his errands, observing his ways and sitting at his feet. He studied him. Here was a man unimpressed by the political establishment. He had taken the measure of the Ahabs and Jezebels of this world and knew of what stuff they were made. Here was a man, moreover, totally unimpressed by the military establishment. Time and again whole companies of soldiers had been sent to arrest him. He simply called down fire from on high to consume them. And he was equally unimpressed by the religious establishment. He had just exposed its error, deception and weakness. Outwardly it seemed powerful, evil and dangerous because it had the backing of the throne. Elijah had exposed it as empty and devoid of spiritual power. As for the school of the prophets, Elijah long since ceased to hope for much from that source. Elijah's hopes and affections were all fixed on things above. Elisha sat at the master's feet and absorbed these things.

Finally, we see the SPIRITUAL HEIR. At length the time came for Elijah to be translated from earth to heaven. He took his journey from Gilgal to Bethel, from Bethel to Jericho and from Jericho to Jordan—the reverse route to that taken by Israel long years ago in its conquest of Canaan. At each stage of the journey, Elijah put his disciple to the test. Each place they came to offered an opportunity and a place of ministry. Again and again, the Master gave his disciple an opportunity to settle down, to settle for less. Each time Elisha said, "No!" He was a man trained to follow the plow, to never take his eye off the goal. And what Elisha wanted was a double portion of the Master's spirit. At all costs. He had not given ten years of his life sitting at Elijah's feet in order to compromise now.

And that is what he received—a double portion of the Master's spirit. Elijah performed eight miracles, Elisha performed sixteen. He was Elijah's spiritual heir.

Henceforth there was to be a man in heaven and a man on earth. The man in heaven had once lived on earth. He had trodden the path of obedience down here. He was now seated on high. The man on earth received a double portion of the Spirit of the man now in heaven. The Master went up, the Spirit came down.

Henceforth the man on earth would tread the same path of obedience once trodden on earth by the man now in heaven.

The whole scene was a foreview of Christ in heaven and Christians on earth. As we live down here the life of the Man up there, we, too, know something of the outpouring of the Spirit of God upon us. "He that believeth on me," Jesus said, "the works that I do shall he do also," and greater works than these.

THE MANTLE OF ELIJAH
II KINGS 2:13-14

Down it came, down from on high, down to the ground to lie in a heap at the feet of Elisha, Elijah's colleague, servant and friend. Elisha picked it up. It was the seal of a new covenant between him and the ascended master in heaven. He had prayed for a double portion of the Master's Spirit. "Keep your eye on me, then," said Elijah. That was what Elisha had done. Now he had the mantle of the Man in the Glory.

Elisha saw something few have ever seen. He saw a living man caught up through the clouds. There had come a mighty rushing wind such as later came at Pentecost. There had come a chariot and horses of fire. Heaven had touched earth for an instant, there at Jordan, the river of death; and the Master was gone. All that remained was a mantle, still warm from the touch of a living man, now caught up into heaven. The crack in the space-time dimension closed, and Elisha stood there alone.

How long Elisha stood there gazing up into heaven we do not know. But presently he brought his gaze back down to earth; and there it was—a mantle, the seal of the new covenant, the earnest of his inheritance. It was now his. And with it came the double portion he had desired. That mantle marked him out as a firstborn son. He picked it up, and the spirit of the master in heaven clothed the body of the disciple on earth. He would walk worthy of his lord. He would be fruitful in every good work. He would increase in the knowledge of God. But let us come back to that mantle.

The mantle of Elijah is mentioned four times. The first time it is associated with the PARADOX of the man of God. For Elijah, mighty man of God that he was, had feet of clay. He was a man subject to like passions as we are. We find him on Horeb, the Mount of God, far from where he belonged. God ministered gently to him. He revealed Himself in the fury of the wind and in the forces of the earthquake and in the fierceness of the fire. Elijah hid in the cave as all nature rumbled, roared and rolled about him. Then came the still small voice. Elijah ventured out, his face wrapped in his mantle, and self-pitying still. We see the man who could call down fire sulking like a schoolboy. Alas, there would be no more Carmels after this. The paradox remains. The greatest man on earth was overcome by passions such as overthrow and then water from heaven. God, most assuredly, does not whitewash the heroes of the faith.

The second time the mantle is mentioned it shows us the PERSONAL-ITY of the man of God. There goes Elisha following his plow. Here comes Elijah, mantle in hand. The prophet throws the mantle over the plowman; and, so great is the power and charisma of Elijah, this successful business-man gives up all to follow him. Of course there wasn't a man, woman, boy or girl from the king on his throne to the mendicant on the city streets, who has not heard of Elijah or been touched by the force of his personality.

The next time that we see that mantle it reminds us of the POWER of a man of God. One flick of that mantle over Jordan's wave, and the waters fled. There was more power in the hem of that garment than in all the robes in King Ahab's house.

We see that mantle one more time, and it reminds us of the PILGRIM-AGE of a man of God. For when his earthly pathway was ended, Elijah stepped into a whirlwind, and was gone. He would need the mantle no more. He passed on to his heir. The new young prophet wore that mantle with all the authority of the one to whom it had formerly belonged.

The Lord expects the same of us. We are Christ's heirs to the Holy Spirit. We wear the Lord's mantle of power. The pilgrim church moves on through time, the mantle of the Spirit of God being the guarantee that God's will will be done on earth, even as it is in heaven.

THE LEPER

A leper! Oh, the horror of it! A leper! It was a doom worse than death. For a while a leper could hide his disease and he could pretend to be well. But it spread. Worse still, it could be caught by others. And there was no cure. All that could be done was to put the leper outside the camp and make him cover his lip and cry "unclean" if anyone came that way. There is a notable difference made between sickness and leprosy in the Bible. Jesus HEALED the sick, the he CLEANED the leper. The Hebrews regarded leprosy as "the stroke of God." There was no hope for the leper. He was unclean and excommunicated and could look forward only to death.

Five Old Testament lepers come to mind. Astonishingly enough, the first leper in Scripture was MOSES! His leprosy was intended to REVEAL to him that he was no better than Pharaoh. Only he had accepted God's grace and Pharaoh had not. Before ever Moses could pronounce judgment on Pharaoh, he had to pronounce judgment on himself. Hand and heart he was a leper in God's sight.

Equally astonishing, the second leper was MIRIAM, the honored sister of Moses. Her leprosy was to REBUKE. She had criticized Moses for marrying an Ethiopian woman, so God smote her. It is a serious thing to speak slightingly of God's servants. Thank to the intercession of Moses, Miriam was healed.

The next leper was NAAMAN. In this case, God intended to RESTORE. Jesus reminded the people of Nazareth that there were many lepers in Israel in the days of Elisha. "None of them was cleansed saving Naaman the Syrian," He said. The people of Nazareth were so enraged at Jesus for speaking these words they tried to murder Him (Lk.4:27-29). The cleansing of Naaman illustrates God's way of salvation. All Naaman's preconceived ideas as to how he would be saved had to be set aside. He had to go to the place appointed by God. He had to accept God's terms, humble his pride and receive salvation as a gift. So do we.

The next leper was GEHAZI. Here the intention was to REPAY. For Gehazi spoiled everything. Elisha had gone to great lengths to teach Naaman that salvation could not be purchased. Gehazi ruined it all by running after the departing Naaman and by asking for money and merchandise in Elisha's name. The prophet's swift judgment was terrible. He smote Gehazi with Naaman's leprosy.

Then came King UZZIAH. This leprosy was intended to RESTRAIN for, swollen with pride and presumption, Uzziah tried to intrude into the priests' office knowing full well that the Law separated between "church" and state. God smote him right there in the Temple, and he remained a leper to the day of his death.

The Levitical code made provision for the cleansing of the leper. Probably, however, the only time it was ever used, throughout the entire Old Testament period, was in the case of Miriam.

The cleansing (Lev.14) revolved around three focal points. First, there was the leper's <u>remarkable condition</u>. Apart from Moses, Miriam, and Naaman, we read of no other leper being cured in Old Testament times. So, it would indeed have been a remarkable thing had one showed up at the house of the nearest priest to announce himself restored—just the very thing Jesus invariably told lepers He cleansed to go and do. (See Matt.8:1-4).

Next, was the leper's <u>ritual cleansing</u>. Once satisfied that the leprosy was gone, the priest took two birds. One of these he killed in an earthen vessel over running water. This pointed to the <u>redemptive</u> work of Christ. The earthen vessel spoke of the Lord's body which was the instrument whereby He suffered death. The running water symbolizes the Holy Spirit for it was "through the eternal Spirit He offered himself without spot unto God." The other bird was dipped in the blood of the first one. The leper was pronounced clean, and the living bird was released to carry the testifying blood up to heaven—pointing to the <u>resurrection</u> and ascension work of Christ.

Finally, we have the leper's <u>restored communion</u>. This took more time and called for a much deeper appreciation of Calvary than that symbolized by the two birds. The cleansed leper was finally allowed back into the camp, but fellowship was not immediately restored. He had to "tarry abroad" (i.e. live out of doors) for seven days. After further ritual cleansing, he was pronounced clean. But then came a most elaborate ritual involving a trespass offering, a sin offering and a burnt offering and the application of the blood (the finished work of Christ) and of the oil (the continuing work of the Spirit) to his extremities. In all this, the priest was prominent (pointing to the unfinished work of Christ as our Great High Priest in heaven). Then, when all was done, the leper was finally declared to be clean. Truly sin (of which leprosy is but a type) is a tenacious thing.

THOU SHALT REMEMBER
DEUTERONOMY 24:18

"Thou shalt remember thou wast a bondman in Egypt, and the Lord thy God redeemed thee. Therefore, when thou cuttest thy field and hast forgot a sheaf in the field, thou shalt not go again to fetch it . . . It shall be for the stranger, the fatherless, the widow."

The Book of Deuteronomy should really be called "<u>Down Memory Lane</u>." Two phrases run side by side through the book: "Thou shalt remember" and "Beware lest ye forget."

Here Moses calls upon God's people to remember three things.

THEIR RUIN "Thou shalt remember thou wast a slave in Egypt." This was John Newton's favorite text. He lived a wild and profligate life on the high seas as a slave trader. Eventually he sank so low as to actually become the slave of a slave, the slave of a Negress who exulted in her power over him and made him even beg for his bread. He could never recall those days without a shudder. After his conversion he wrote out this text—"Thou shalt remember thou wast a bondsman (a slave) . . . and the Lord thy God redeemed thee." He put it on the mantelpiece of his study to remind him.

But, back to Israel's plight in Egypt. A slave! In Egypt! How indeed had the mighty fallen! Proud Judah, crafty Levi, cruel Simeon, ambitious Ephraim, slaves, all of them. And under the sentence of death, with no power to redeem themselves, still less to redeem their brother. Such was the extent of their ruin.

Then, too, they were to remember THEIR REDEMPTION: "The LORD thy God redeemed thee." The Lord, Jehovah that is, the <u>God of Covenant</u>. Jehovah, the One Who had entered into a contractual relationship with Abraham in what we now call the Abrahamic Covenant. And what a covenant! An unconditional contract embracing the promulgation, protection and promotion of Abraham's seed. "The LORD redeemed thee!"—He was faithful to His contract despite their unfaithfulness.

"The Lord thy GOD redeemed thee." God! This time the word is Elohim—God as the God of creation, the God Who has power enough and to spare. What a God He is! He has power to endow an atom with energy enough to annihilate an island of the sea. The God Who has power enough to fuel a hundred billion stars in a hundred billion galaxies and send them on prodigious journeys at unconceivable velocities across the vast reaches of space.

"The LORD thy GOD redeemed thee," Moses said. "Never forget it!" Rather, "Never forget HIM."

Moreover, they were to remember THEIR RESPONSIBILITY. They were to express their gratitude, not in sacrifices and offerings, not in rituals and religious observances, though, of course, such things had their place. They were to remember it by showing kindness to the poor, to the widow, to the stranger and to the fatherless. And especially at harvest time.

God would have us to be ever mindful of the poor. He is mindful of them for when His own Son lived down here on earth, He was Himself numbered among the poor. We should never forget it.

SATAN'S POWER
LUKE 10:19

The word for total, absolute power in the New Testament is <u>dunamis</u> (from which we get our English word "dynamite". Before the resurrection of Christ, Satan wielded this power. The Lord, for instance, spoke of "all the power (<u>dunamis</u>) of the enemy" (Lk.10:19).

In this age, however, Satan's power has been curbed. The kind of power Satan once had (<u>dunamis</u>) has now been given to the Church. The Lord told His disciples: "Ye shall receive power (<u>dunamis</u>) after that the Holy Ghost is come upon you" (Acts 1:8). In writing to the Church at Rome, Paul declared, "I am not ashamed of the gospel of Christ for it is the power (<u>dunamis</u>) of God unto salvation to everyone that believeth" (Rom. 1:16).

So, although Satan wields tremendous power, the fact remains that all his power is under restraint. The Holy Spirit restrains him, holds him back, and, at times, administers major setbacks to his plans by sending revival to the Church. "Greater is He that is in you," Jesus said, "than he that is in the world." Satan is no match for the Holy Spirit of God.

In this present age Satan's power is described by the word <u>exosuia</u>. The word suggests delegated authority. At His return the Lord Jesus is going to put down all rule and authority (1 Cor. 15:24). Satan, today, is "the prince of the power (authority) of the air." We, as believers, have been delivered from the power (authority) of darkness and have been translated into the kingdom of God's dear Son (Col. 1:13). Paul was commissioned to turn people from the power (authority) of Satan unto God (Acts 26:18). Jesus came to destroy the works of the devil (1 John 3:8).

After the rapture of the Church, Satan will receive back his <u>dunamis</u> his ancient power, that will enable him to bring in his agent, the Antichrist. When this ominous person is revealed his coming will be "after the working of Satan with all power (<u>dunamis</u>) and signs and lying wonders" (2 Thess. 2:9). His hour of triumph will be spectacular. He will succeed in bringing the whole world under his control. But his day will be short. The Lord, at His coming to reign, will put an end to Satan's long-sought, short-lived triumph on this earth.

"He must reign," Paul says of Christ. Of course, He must! This world was the scene of His rejection, and it is going to be the scene of His glory and power. He will reign in righteousness on the very plant where He was cast out and crucified for a thousand years.

At the end of that reign, Satan, incarcerated in the Abyss for its entire period will be released long enough to lead a final, massive revolt against Christ. Millions of people will be born in the Millennial age. Large numbers of them will be born again and will become heirs of the kingdom. Countless others, however, will NOT be born again. They will long to indulge their natural lusts but will fear the long arm of the Lord. The Psalmist tells us that the Lord will rule this planet with "a rod of iron" (Ps. 2). Satan will find these unregenerate malcontents willing tools for his final revolt. "Then cometh the end," (<u>telos</u>, the very end) Paul says. Satan's revolt will be crushed. The world will be disintegrated and replaced by a new heaven and a new earth. The wicked dead, of all the ages, will be raised, judged and banished to a lost eternity. All things will now come under Christ's control. Once all things are subdued by Christ, "then shall the Son also Himself be subject unto Him that put all things under Him that God may be all in all" ("everything to everyone" is the way it has been rendered—1 Cor.15:28). What a day of rejoicing that will be.

THE ROAD TO ENDOR
I SAMUEL 28:1-25

It was a long, perilous, evil road from Ramah, where the prophet Samuel lived, to the place where the witch of Endor lived. Of course, she had no business living there, or anywhere else, for the Mosaic law decreed that witches be put to death. But live she did, and the path to her door was the path which

King Saul trod. It took him forty years to get there, and it cost him dear when he did. The milestones he passed on that long, winding, downward road still mark out the way. There are a half dozen of them all told.

The first milestone marked Saul's UNDEVELOPED POTENTIAL (11-12). He seems to have cut an impressive figure in his younger days and was chosen by the people to be king because he looked so very much a man. And he started well enough, rescuing the city of Jabesh-gilead from the power of the Ammonite king. The victory encouraged the aging Samuel to retire, for Saul, it seemed, had the potential to be a good king. Sadly, he allowed it to all go to waste.

The second milestone marked Saul's UNPARDONABLE PRESUMP-TION (13). War broke out with the Philistines. The aged Samuel promised to come and bless Saul's men and set a time for doing so. The appointed week wore on. Men began to desert, and still Samuel tarried. Saul felt he was losing his army and became impatient so he took it on himself to act as priest. If Samuel wanted to dilly-dally then that was too bad for Samuel. Saul intruded into the priests' exclusive domain and sacrificed his offering himself. It never seemed to occur to him that God was testing him by Samuel's Divinely appointed delay. The smoke was still ascending from his altar when Samuel appeared. He denounced Saul and told him he had forfeited the kingdom. Moreover, God had Saul's successor in mind, "a man after God's own heart."

The third milestone marked Saul's UNTIMELY PROCRASTINA-TION (14). The desultory war with the Philistines needed to be brought to a head, but Saul had no stomach for fighting Philistines. So Jonathan, Saul's son, took the lead. What was King Saul doing? He was tarrying, we are told, in the uttermost part of Gibea, under a pomegranate tree. He was wasting his time. He had failed once by precipitation. He failed now by procrastination.

The fourth milestone marked his UNSATISFACTORY PERFOR-MANCE (15). The time had come to visit God's judgment on the Amalakites for their bitter hostility to the people of God. "Slay utterly," was God's command. They must deal with this relentless foe once and for all. (In Bible typology Amalek represents the flesh. God tells us to deal with it as drastically as Saul was to deal with Amalek).

Saul triumphed, indeed, but he spared Agag the Amalekite king and the best of the flocks and herds. Saul had failed another test. Samuel angrily brushed off Saul's excuses. He called him a rebel. "Rebellion is as the sin of witchcraft," said Samuel, with a prophetic eye on the future and final fate of King Saul. Truly this was a notable milestone. The incident marked the end of any further Divine validity to Saul's reign and to the beginning of a life of crime.

The fifth milestone marked his UNDISGUISED PARALYSIS. The Philistines declared war and put forth their giant, Goliath. He challenged Saul, (a giant himself) to come and fight him man to man. Saul shook in his shoes. He was so petrified with terror he let a young lad, David by name, go and fight the giant for him. The people soon sized up that act of cowardice.

The sixth milestone marked his UNREMITTING PERSECUTION of the one who had taken his place in the valley of death. No less than twenty-four times King Saul tried to kill David. One black day, he massacred a whole company of priests, accusing them of high treason because their leader had given David some small loaves of bread and Goliath's sword, to help him out of the country.

And so, at last, King Saul came to Endor where lived a witch. Samuel was dead. Heaven was silent when he prayed. And once again the Philistines were preparing to invade. The new, puppet high priest Saul had installed could get no answer from God, either, when he tried to intercede. So Saul turned to the witch. He had knocked on heaven's door in vain. He decided to knock instead on the door of Hell. God opened that door suddenly and startlingly. Instead of the witch's familiar spirit showing up the dead Samuel did—to sentence Saul to death. So, having opened a normally barred and bolted door, God pushed Saul through it to a lost eternity.

Centuries later the hireling prophet, Balaam, said: "Let me die the death of the righteous and let my latter and be like his." He, too, died under the judgment of God. For we cannot die the death of the righteous if we do not live the life of the righteous. And that King Saul never did.

A VERY POPULAR TEXT
JOHN 3:16

The Holy Spirit sums up God's work in <u>creating</u> in ten statements: "And God said . . ." (Gen.1). He sums up God's Word in <u>legislation</u> in ten commandments (Ex.20). And here, in John 3:16, He sums up God's way of <u>salvation</u> in ten words: GOD - LOVED - WORLD - GAVE - SON - WHOSOEVER - BELIEVETH - PERISH - HATH - LIFE. Just ten words to tell us how to live forever. They can be grouped into five pairs.

THE SOURCE OF SALVATION. We notice first, <u>The Giver</u>: "God." The Greek word is <u>Theos</u>, the word used in the Greek Bible for the God of the Old Testament—for Elohim, the God Who Creates, for Jehovah, the God Who Covenants, and Adonai, the God Who Commands. Such is the Giver. The question of human sin and of man's salvation did not take God by surprise. God had thought it all out before ever He fashioned Adam's clay.

Next, we have <u>the Gift</u>. God did not give an angel to be our savior. The One Who came from heaven to accomplish our salvation was co-equal, co-eternal and co-existent with the Father and the Spirit. He was uncreated and self-existent. He was omnipotent, omniscient and omnipresent. He was the Second Person of the Godhead. That is the One Who came into the world to save sinners. No wonder Paul teaches us to say: "Thanks be unto God for His unspeakable gift" (2 Cor.9:15). It is, perhaps, just an incident of translation; but there are twenty-five words in John 3:16 and the center one is SON. God makes His Son the center of everything.

THE SECRET OF IT ALL. Here we have first <u>the great reality</u>—"God Loved." When young Henry Morehouse preached for a week in D.L. Moody's church in Chicago years ago he preached every night on this text. He finished with these words: "I have been trying to tell you how much God loves you. If I could borrow Jacob's ladder and climb to the city of God and ask Gabriel, the herald angel, to tell me how much God loves the world, He would say: 'God so loved the world He gave His only begotten Son . . .'"

Next, we have <u>the great result</u>—"God so loved . . . He <u>gave</u> His only begotten Son." Salvation was to be so simple to obtain that anyone, man or woman, boy or girl, rich or poor, wise or foolish, could make it their very own. So God offers it to us as a free and unconditional gift. All we have to do to receive a gift, and make it our own, is to accept it. All the world's false religions say that salvation has to be earned. God says that salvation is free.

THE SIMPLICITY OF IT ALL. First we have the response of faith. "Whosoever believeth . . ." Everyone has the capacity to believe, to exercise faith. We exercise faith every day—when we post a letter, when we deposit money in the bank, when we board a plane. Everyday, ordinary faith, such as we exercise in a doctor, a druggist or a driver becomes saving faith when it becomes faith in our Lord Jesus Christ.

Next, we have the reward of faith: "Hath!" The moment we believe, that moment we have eternal life. God says so. There are no conditions, there is no probation, there are no strings attached. It is instantaneous and eternal. "Hath!"

THE SCOPE OF IT ALL. The promise applies to all people universally. . . . "For God so loved the world . . ." The Jews of Jesus' day thought God only loved them, that they had some kind of a monopoly on God. Not so! It is for everyone. As the old children's chorus puts it:

> "Red or yellow, black or white,
> All are precious in His sight."

The promise also applies to all people individually: "That whosoever believeth in Him . . ." The response of the little lad, when he was asked what the word "whosoever" meant, is delightful. He said: "It sort of means everyone else, and me." That, indeed, is the scope of it.

THE SERIOUSNESS OF IT ALL. There is the possibility of ending up in hell. Mark that word "perish." It is a strong word in the Greek. It means "to be lost in utter spiritual destitution." The word is used of the bursting of a wine cask. It implies "utter, incredible loss." No wonder this issue of salvation is so serious.

But there is also the prospect of ending up in heaven: "Shall have everlasting life." That does not just mean length of days. One of Sir Henry Rider Haggard's most popular novels tells of a woman who lengthened her days for two thousand years—and spent them in misery. God offers us, not just a mere quantity of days, but life! Life marked by "joy unspeakable and full of glory!" His kind of life! What a prospect!

THE LORD'S SUPPER
1 CORINTHIANS 11:23-34

Public worship reaches its climax at the Lord's table, as we partake of the emblems on the table. We do so in remembrance of the Lord Jesus, and because He requests it.

Exhorting one another in the things of God is not worship. Singing and special music do not in themselves constitute worship. Reciting specially chosen Scripture passages is not in itself worship. Following a carefully planned order of service does not guarantee worship. Listening to pulpit oratory is not worship. Praying for one another does not constitute worship. Being occupied with evangelism, soul-winning, missionary activity and the like does not constitute worship. Though, of course, all these things may at times be elements of worship.

True worship is brought into true focus at the Lord's table. There we are "occupied with no man save Jesus only." That is worship.

At the Lord's table, we remember the Lord, in Spirit and in truth (Jno. 4:24). That, of course, excludes all those who do not know Him. You cannot remember someone you do not know and have never met. Occupation with the Lord Jesus reaches its climax in partaking of the bread and of the wine. This is pure worship. It should be spontaneous, not arranged. It should be guided in all its parts (a carefully chosen and appropriate hymn here, a relevant Scripture reading there, with or without comment, now a prayer of praise and adoration, in keeping with the occasion) by the Holy Spirit.

Three elements are prominent in such worship. Paul reminds us that we are to be taken up with the Lord's PERSON. Jesus, in instituting this feast of remembrance, said, "This do in remembrance of Me." That opens up a vast field of worship. We can be taken up with the Lord's deity, with His humanity, His attributes and His wisdom, with His love and power. We can be occupied with His Eternal preexistence as God the Son, second Person of the Godhead. We can worship Him as Creator of the universe, the One Who is adored and served by all the angel throng.

We can remember He is truly Man. We can meditate on His incarnation, His life, His words and works, His death, burial and resurrection, His oneness with the Father and with the Spirit and with His bride. All these and many other things involved in remembering His Person.

More, we are to be taken up with the Lord's PASSION: "As often as ye eat this bread and drink this cup ye do show the Lord's death . . ." This, too, opens up a vast field of worship. Many Old Testament types remind us of His death. The various offerings, for instance, the feasts, truths connected with the tabernacle, and its furniture. Such monumental passages as Psalm 22, Psalm 69 and Isaiah 53 all come to mind. So do the frequent references to the Lord's death in the Gospels and epistles. We focus in worship on the events which surrounded the Lord's death, burial and resurrection. We think of His sufferings, the events of His last crowded week on earth. We stand with Moses and Elijah on the holy mount as they talk with Him about His decease. He stand in Pilate's judgment hall. We journey from Gethsemane to Gabbatha to Golgotha and the grave. We remember His passion. Besides our open Bibles, a hundred hymns help us to do.

But there is one thing more. We are to be taken up with the Lord's POSITION. For we remember Him thus "till He comes." The Lord is no longer on the cross or in the tomb. He is seated at the right hand of the majesty on high. He is our Advocate with the Father. He is our great High Priest. He is coming again. All these things provide us with themes for worship.

Worship, after all, is the ascription of worthship to Him.

FOREKNOWN

ROMANS 8:29-30

The passage moves us steadily forward from a dateless, timeless past to an endless, eternal prospect in ages yet unborn but yet to be—Foreknown! Predestinated! Called! Justified! Glorified! Mark the onward march of the words—Five movements in a monumental process all initiated by God. We are brought:

INTO THE SPHERE OF HIS WISDOM—"Foreknown!" It goes without saying that since God is omniscient, since He knows everything, He knows the future as well as the past. Our knowledge is after-knowledge. We know things <u>after</u> they have happened. God's knowledge is <u>fore</u>-knowledge. God can know things <u>before</u> they happen. Both kinds of knowledge depend on the fact that certain things happen. It is a matter of perspective.

As we live our lives, we establish all kinds of facts about ourselves. They are written indelibly into our personal history—the date of our birth, our circumstances, our decisions, the date of our conversion, the date of our death. All these, and a myriad others, besides, are facts we establish as we live our lives. After-knowledge (our kind of knowledge) sees these facts and writes them down as <u>history</u>. God sees the same facts and writes them down also as <u>prophecy</u>. So, we are foreknown. God brings us into the sphere of His wisdom.

We are brought UNDER THE SOVEREIGNTY OF HIS WILL. We are "<u>predestinated</u>!" Based upon His foreknowledge of our acceptance of Christ, God determined certain things for us, all those things which accompany salvation. Specifically, Paul tells us that God predetermines that every child of His will one day be like Jesus. In fact, so strong is this determination, in God's mind, it is already done. We <u>are</u> going to be conformed to the image of His Son. God has sovereignly decreed it. We are predestinated to that end. Nothing can prevent it. All things will work together to ensure it. The word which declares it is in the past tense. So far as God is concerned, it is already done.

We are brought UNDER THE SOUND OF HIS WORD. We are "<u>called</u>!" God's call is universal. Paul reminded the men of Athens that God "commandeth <u>all men</u>, <u>everywhere</u> to repent." God does not close the Bible until three times in one short verse. He issues a universal call—"Come!" "Come!" "Come!" But that call becomes effective only when we respond. When Adam and Eve sinned, God called. In time, both responded. Adam declared his faith at once. He called his wife, Eve, "the mother of all living." Eve declared her faith at a later date. She called her firstborn, Cain, and confessed her belief in the promise of God. "I have gotten the Man," she said, "even Jehovah." So God calls, and man responds.

We are brought UNDER THE SHADOW OF HIS WILL. We are "<u>justified</u>!" Justification is a much better thing than mere forgiveness. In order to be forgiven, a person has to plead guilty. You cannot pardon an innocent man. To be justified means that you are so declared righteous by God that the Law, even God Himself, can find no ground for impeachment. When we are saved God can find no ground for impeachment. When we are saved God puts us "in Christ." When He looks at us, He sees Him and all His righteousness. So He declares us to be righteous, justified!

We are brought INTO THE SPLENDOR OF HIS WORLD. We are "glorified!" This, also, is in the past tense. It is in the future, so far as we are concerned; but it is already done, so far as God is concerned. "Eye hath not seen," says Paul, "nor ear heard the things which God has prepared for them that love Him." There lies ahead for us what Paul calls "an exceeding and eternal weight of glory" (2 Cor.4:17). Blessed be God our God!

NO FOE! NO FEAR!

ROMANS 8:35-39

In concluding his treatise on the eternal security of the believer, Paul tells us two things. He tells us that no foe can daunt us (35-37).

Think of the long list of Paul's sufferings which he lists in Corinthians—prison sentences, beatings, stonings, shipwrecks. The list goes on and on. "In all these things," he was, "more than conqueror."

Or look at Peter, imprisoned by Herod, sentenced to death, scheduled to be executed on the morrow. What is he doing? Bemoaning his fate? No! Is he facing his cell, summoning his resolve, vowing to die like a man? NO! He is asleep! He is not only conqueror, he is more than conqueror. No foe can daunt him, not even the monstrous Herod who ruled his little world. Then, too, No Fear Can Haunt Us (38-39) Paul parades a host of possibilities for our inspection, all of them potential disturbers of our peace.

There is the inevitable. Death awaits us all. It is the King of Terrors. It separates friend from friend, husband from wife, mother from child. Can death separate us from the love of God? Of course not! Jesus has conquered death and all its powers. He says: "Behold I am alive forevermore! I have the keys of death and hell" (Rev.1:18).

There is the invisible. Can invisible angels disturb our peace? Can principalities and powers separate us from God's love? No! Among the ranks of the angels, there are thrones and dominions (angelic beings loyal to God);

and there are "principalities and powers" (angelic beings loyal to Satan). There are the rulers of this world's darkness, and there are wicked spirits in high places. All have been utterly shattered and defeated by Christ at Calvary and are now chained to the chariot wheels of His triumph (Col.2:15).

There is the inescapable. "Can things present separate us from God's love?" Obviously not because Jesus is ever present. He says: "Lo I am with you always, even to the end of the world" (Matt.28:20). To get at us, those things which might haunt us have to get past Him. As for things to come, He is the coming One and is so portrayed from Genesis to Revelation. Well might we sing:

> *"Midst the darkness, storm and sorrow*
> *One bright gleam I see*
> *Well I know that on the morrow*
> *Christ will come for me."*

Moreover, "in the ages to come" God intends to show us "the exceeding riches of His grace in His kindness through Christ Jesus" (Eph.2:7).

There is the INCALCULABLE—Can height or depth haunt us or harm us? No indeed! Christ is not only at home in the heights, He has put them beneath our feet. We are already seated with Him in heavenly places (Eph.1:21). As for the depths, He has been down to the bottom, down to "the lower parts of the earth" (Eph.4:9-10) and has been down there as Conqueror, as the Mighty victor over sin and death and Hell. There is nothing for us to fear down there. He has made sure of that.

Finally, there is the INCONCEIVABLE. What about "any other creature?" There is no creature on earth, no creature in the highest heavens, or in the deepest depths, no creature unknown or unimagined, that can harm us. Because He has created all things and all creatures bend at last before His will and own Him to be their Lord. Creatures unknown may have vast power, But He has omnipotent power.

Nothing can separate us from the love of "Jesus Christ our Lord." That phrase is Paul's closing word in Romans five successive chapters in Romans, chapters five, six, seven and eight. In chapter five Jesus Christ our Lord separates. In chapter six Jesus Christ our Lord saves. In chapter seven Jesus Christ our Lord sanctifies, and in chapter eight Jesus Christ our Lord secures. Hallelujah! What a Savior!

EETERNAL SECURITY
ROMANS 8:28-39

In the closing section of his great treatise on the Christian life (Rom.8), Paul deals with the security of the believer. We are <u>predestined</u> for <u>glory</u> (28-30), and we are <u>preserved</u> for <u>glory</u> (31-39). God knows all about us. Nothing happens by chance. Paul says: "We know that all things work together for good to them that love God, to them who are the called according to His purpose."

Here we have <u>a blessed assurance</u>. Paul says, "We know." We do not have to indulge in wishful thinking. God has spoke, and His Word cannot be broken. We have, moreover, <u>a basic assumption</u>. God says: "all things work together for good to them that love God, to them who are the called according to His purpose. All things work together for everyone, for better or for worse. All things work together for <u>good</u> for those who are <u>His people</u> and those who are in <u>His purpose</u>. Jacob, the Old Testament patriarch, shows us how all this works out in the end.

We see him sitting in his tent, wringing his hands with grief. A great cry of despair breaks from his lips. Ever since he returned to the Promised Land, everything seems to have gone wrong. If any man was a man "called according to God's purpose," Jacob was that man. He was back in the Land, back to the place where God had put His Name and where He met with His people. But everything seems to have conspired against him.

He had narrowly escaped being plundered by Laban, his unscrupulous father-in-law. He had purchased his peace with Esau at great price, even though he could not be sure that Esau might not yet be back for more, backed by his four hundred fighting men. His only daughter has been seduced and disgraced; and his sons, Simeon and Levi, have wreaked fearful vengeance on the man responsible. They have put the whole family in peril. His beloved, Rachel, has died; and his dear Joseph has disappeared and presumed to be dead, torn to pieces by wild beasts. Judah, the best of a bad lot, has disgraced himself. A famine is raging in the Promised Land, and keeping the family together requires that his sons go back to Egypt to buy more corn. Already his son, Simeon, has been detained in Egypt by the imperious Grand Vizier.

Worse still, that despotic man has demanded that Benjamin be brought to Egypt as a hostage. Food is needed. The boys must go back for more, but they adamantly refuse to go back for more grain without Benjamin.

"All these things are against me," Jacob wailed. Little did he know that all things were working together for good! Joseph was alive and seated at the right hand of power in Egypt, the very Grand Vizier he dreads. Simeon is living off the fat of the land in Egypt. Soon the wagons will be coming to bring Jacob to Joseph's side. As the hymnwriter would phrase it:

"Ye saints of God fresh courage take,
The clouds ye so much dread
Are big with mercies and shall fall
In blessings on your head."

Yes, indeed! All things do work together for good for those who love God and who are wrapped up in His eternal purpose to bless His own! Dark as things may seem, there is another side to our circumstances—God's side:

"Not till the looms are silent
And the shuttles cease to fly,
Will God unroll the fabric
And explain the reason why;
The dark threads are as needful
In the Weaver's skillful hand
As the threads of gold and silver
In the pattern He has planned."

THE GROANING OF THE COMFORTER
ROMANS 8:26-27

In his great treatise on the Christian life in Romans 8, Paul tells us of the groaning of the <u>Comforter</u>, of the groaning of the <u>creation</u> and of the groaning of the <u>Christian</u>. Here, it is the Holy Spirit he has in mind, the One the Lord Jesus called "the Comforter." Think of it! The third person of the Godhead <u>groaning</u>. But that is what sin does. Hosea reminds us that sin not only breaks God's laws, it break's God's heart.

The word for groaning is <u>stenagmos</u>. It is used to describe the groanings of the Hebrew slaves in Egypt (Acts 7:34). The word is used in Romans 8 to describe the groaning of the Holy Spirit. It points to an inward, unexpressed feeling. Significantly, the word, used here of the Comforter, is in the plural, intensifying the anguish.

Paul first sets before us <u>revealed truth about prayer</u>. He reminds us of two things. First, <u>how helpless we are</u>: "We know not what to pray for as we ought" and <u>how helpful He is</u>: "Likewise the Spirit also helpeth our infirmities." Most church prayer meetings reveal how inadequate many of our prayers are. Prayer requests seem to consist of a long roll call of the sick, the sad and the suffering. The Lord's prayers and Paul's prayers are occupied mostly with spiritual rather than physical or material things.

The Holy Spirit "helpeth," Paul says. The word is used in Luke 10:40 by Martha when she needed some down-to-earth help in the kitchen. Annoyed that she was tied to the kitchen while her sister Mary sat in the shade talking with Jesus and His disciples, Martha said to the Lord, "Bid her therefore that she <u>help</u> me." It is no accident, surely, that the very name "Comforter" is "<u>Paraclete</u>," One "called alongside to help."

We have, here, too, not only revealed truth about prayer, but also <u>real travail in prayer</u>. "The Spirit Himself maketh intercession for us with groanings which cannot be uttered." J. B. Phillips paraphrases that: "His Spirit within us is actually praying for us in those agonizing longings which cannot be uttered."

But there is more! We have here <u>remarkable triumph in prayer</u>. "He that searcheth the hearts knoweth what is in the mind of the Spirit because He maketh intercession according to the will of God."

In other words, the Holy Spirit <u>knows my heart</u>. "He searcheth the hearts." He can read us like a book. He sees:

"The secret springs,
The motives that control;
Those places where polluted things
Hold empire o'er the soul."

He knows us better than we know ourselves. Then, too, He <u>knows His own mind</u>. "He knoweth what is the mind of the Spirit." He has already made up His mind about every situation in which we find ourselves and never makes mistakes. Finally, He <u>knows God's will</u>—"He maketh intercession according to the will of God." Therefore, it is absolutely impossible for the Holy Spirit ever to ask for a wrong thing or ever to get a "<u>No</u>!" answer. How wonderful that He is <u>on</u> our side, and <u>by</u> our side, at all times.

IT WAS GOOD

GENESIS 1

God is good—absolutely good. It is impossible for Him to do anything bad. The imprint of His goodness lies on all He does. It is evident, for instance, in every step and every stage of the work of creation as recorded in Genesis 1.

Out there in space, the vast machinery of the universe pulsated and roared, swirling around the great white throne of God. Countless billions of stars and their satellites were hurrying through intangible space on prodigious orbits at inconceivable velocities and with mathematical precision. God made it all, and it was all good. The angels of God around His throne shouted and sang in awe and wonder at this display of omniscient wisdom and omnipotent power.

Somewhere, in the midst of this sublime activity, there swirled a galaxy of some 100 billion stars, a galaxy we call the Milky Way. One of those stars was unique, we call it the sun. It had gathered around it a solar system of planets. One of those planets we call the Earth.

It was a world in need of repair. For some reason, barely hinted at in Scripture, this planet was "without form and void" and darkness concealed the face of the deep. It was about to become the platform, however, on which God would stage a demonstration of the fact that He is good as well as great.

"Light be!" He said. And instantly light was. Just like that! Light reigned. And it was good as God is good. The light revealed a chaos of tossing water, a vast and shoreless sea. No land raised its head above the heaving waves and smothering mist. God called for an atmosphere to be formed. At once, two vast oceans appeared, one above and one below, with a far-flung firmament between, a space for clouds to congregate, a playground for weather to have its way. God said that it was good.

But still the rolling seas held restless empire over all the world. God put an instant end to that. The continents arose, towering peaks appeared and the land threw off the mantle of the sea. And it was good.

Then life arose in countless varieties and forms. The seas swarmed with life. The sky was taken over by birds and other creatures made with wings. Vegetation threw a garment of green over vast segments of the earth. Forests sprang up everywhere. Creatures great and small grazed the glens and roamed the vast forests of a pristine world. And it was good.

Then God made man, made him in His own image and after His own likeness, made him to be inhabited by God Himself. He was to be a creature apart, able to think and feel and decide, able to speak and sing, able to appreciate beauty, and control his environment, and rule the world and worship God. And it was good. Everything was good. In fact, it was very good. God said so. And so it was. The word the Holy Spirit uses for "good" means "beautiful." The Holy Spirit used it seven times in telling us the tale.

And then God said, "It is not good!" For though Adam was monarch of all he surveyed, though all things were under his feet, though he was indwelt by God and though he loved God and obeyed God and had daily fellowship with God, he ruled his vast empire alone. The birds of the air had companions to share their nests. The foxes had mates to share their dens. Only Adam roamed the world alone. It was not good.

So God went to work again. One day Adam awoke from a deep sleep, and what he saw must have made him think he was still asleep or in a dream! For there she stood, his counterpart, the woman God had especially made for him. And suddenly everything was good. God is good—that was what it all said. Far-flung galaxies, creatures from the seas and skies, all of nature has one song to sing:

"How good is the God we adore,
Our faithful unchangeable Friend,
Whose love is as great as His power,
And knows neither measure nor end."

"YE MUST BE BORN AGAIN"

JOHN 3

The words shook Nicodemus to the core of his being. They cut through his opening pleasantries in which he conceded that God was with the young prophet from Nazareth. The words cut through his conscientious philanthropies, his tithes, his offerings, his contributions to the poor. The words shattered his religious priorities, fasting, keeping the law, working his way to heaven. "Except a man be born again," Jesus declared, "he cannot see the kingdom of God."

But, first, let us look at THE MAN. He was rich. His contribution to the burial of Christ, for instance, was a hundred pounds of costly spices, a fortune, far beyond anything an ordinary working man could afford.

He was respected as "a ruler of the Jews," a member of the Sanhedrin, the chief governing body of the nation.

He was religious, being a member of the sect of Pharisees, fanatics for the letter of the law. Surely, he said to himself, if any man deserved to go to heaven, I do. His credentials were impeccable. He had spent his whole life climbing the religious ladder. Now, belatedly, he discovered it was leaning against the wrong wall. Such was the man, the very finest product of self-righteous religion.

What troubled him was THE MESSAGE. Jesus had just informed him that what he needed was a new birth, a new beginning altogether. Curiously enough, religious though he was, the Lord's words struck an unsuspected responsive chord. He did not say, "Why?" He said, "How?" He said: "How can a man be born when he is old?" Can we not detect a note of longing in those words? Nicodemus was an honest man. He knew how far short he had come of the glory of God. All his almsgiving and zeal for the law and religious observances notwithstanding, he knew that something was missing. His goodness was only relative goodness, he compared favorably when he measured himself alongside men like the publican, the harlot and the thief. But God demanded absolute goodness. Yes, indeed! To be born again, to become as an innocent babe, that was it! But how?

Which brings us to THE MESSAGE. Nicodemus needed to be "born of water and of the Spirit." The Lord's reference to water clearly pointed to the well-known baptism of John, a baptism of repentance. Nicodemus had not submitted to that baptism. The Pharisees, as a group, had officially rejected both John and his baptism. They wrapped their religious robes about them and shuddered at the thought of taking their place in the water as sinners. Not for a single moment could they imagine themselves taking their place in the line to confess their need for repentance and to submit to being baptized by John.

The Lord's references to the baptism of the Spirit underlined Nicodemus' need to be regenerated, to be born again by the Holy Spirit. What he needed was new life, spiritual life. He needed to receive the life of God which could only be imparted by the Holy Spirit to a humbly, repentant man. So, there was the message.

Finally, there was THE METHOD. "But how?" insisted the Pharisee. "Can a man enter into his mother's womb and be reborn?" The Lord explained: "As Moses lifted up the serpent in the wilderness (a reference to an Old Testament incident well-known to Nicodemus), so must the Son of Man be lifted up" (a reference to the Lord's coming crucifixion). Nicodemus saw it at once.

In the Old Testament story, the unbelieving Israelites in the wilderness had been bitten by serpents. There was no medical remedy, and they were dying in droves. At God's command, Moses made a brass serpent and fastened it to a pole. Then he lifted it up for all to see. "Look, and live!" he said. That was all it took—a look of faith. No good works were required, no religious ceremony, no supposed personal merit—just a look! That was the story, and here was its meaning: Jesus would be lifted up as the Sinbearer. More! He would be "made sin." All that was needed, to live forever, was to look in simple faith to Him. A few short years later, Nicodemus saw Christ lifted up on the cross. And that was it! He looked! He lived! He was born again.

HOW CAN A MAN BE BORN WHEN HE IS OLD?

JOHN 3:4

It was a startled old man who asked the question: "How can a man be born when he is old?" The young prophet from Nazareth had shaken him to the core. We gather some information about him right from the start. We know he was rich, respected and religious. Edersheim tells of a Nicodemus who is mentioned in the Talmud, as one of the richest and most distinguished citizens of Jerusalem. There is no actual proof, however, that he was this Nicodemus. Still, our Nicodemus was rich enough to lavishly supply costly spices, later on, for the Lord's burial. Moreover, he was a member of the Sanhedrin, the self-governing body which, under the Romans was allowed to make and administer certain civic and religious laws.

Nicodemus came to Jesus, a daring thing to do. The Lord had just cleansed the temple of its concessions, an act which was tantamount to an open declaration of war with the Jewish authorities. Nicodemus was even willing to go so far as to own Jesus to be "a teacher sent from God," but he could not have been prepared for Jesus' uncompromising and revolutionary reply to his opening remarks. "Except a man be born again," Jesus said, "he cannot see the kingdom of God." A dozen words and Jesus swept away the very foundations of this old man's hopes of heaven. "How can a man be born when he is old?" he said. The words, though they startled Nicodemus, nevertheless struck a responsive chord in the old man's soul, and awoke in him a recognition of a deep need of something better than the legalism in which he had been raised. So much so that, instead of arguing about it, he at once asked how a man could experience a new birth. The Lord had put an unerring finger on his deepest, spiritual need. It was a need he felt, but one that hitherto he had not been able to express. "How?" he said, "How?" He asked the question twice.

How indeed? Later on, when John wrote his gospel, he reduced the Lord's answer to a formula (John 1:11-13).

First, He tells us what being born again is NOT. It is <u>not of blood</u>. That is to say it is <u>not of human descent</u>. Spiritual life is not something we inherit from our parents, however godly. All we inherit from them is a fallen Adamic nature. More, it is <u>not of the will of the flesh</u>. That is, it is <u>not of human desire</u>. A desire to be a member of God's family does not make one a child of God. A desire to be born a member of the royal family does not make one a child of a king. Then, too, it is <u>not of the will of man</u>. That is to say it is <u>not of human determination</u>. No amount of resolve can bring it to pass. A person might say: "Resolved! I consider myself a member of the British royal family." Such a resolve would be completely foolish. To be a member of the British royal family, one must be born into the royal family. Similarly, to be a child of God, one must be born into God's family. He must be born again.

Now look at what being born again IS. First, there is something we have to <u>believe</u>. We must "believe on His Name." And what is His Name? Jesus, of course! And that name simply means "Savior"—"One Who saves His people from their sins" (Matt. 1:21). That is what we need, someone who can save us from sin's penalty, from its power and ultimately from its very presence.

Then comes the next step. It is not enough to "believe." We must also <u>receive</u>. It is one thing for me to believe that Jesus is <u>the</u> Savior, it is another thing for me to know Him as <u>my</u> Savior. That happens when I "receive Him," by asking Him to come into our life.

I <u>believe</u>! I <u>receive</u>! That is our part. Then God says, "<u>Become</u>!" That is His part. The believing and receiving is what we have to do. Then God does what He alone can do, impart to us spiritual life, His life, the life of God; and we are instantly born into His family. We become a child of God. His Holy Spirit comes into our human spirit, and we are born again, born of God.

Things Angels Desire To Look Into (1)
I Peter 1:11-12

"Of which things," says Peter, "the angels desire to look into." One would have thought that they already had enough things to look into—

managing and directing all God's vast empires in space! But no! Their attention has been caught. And no wonder! For, first, God the Son vacated heaven for earth; and, as soon as He came back, God the Holy Spirit did the same.

This desire among the angels is no passing whim. The word the Holy Spirit uses for "desire" means "to desire earnestly." The words "look into" suggest stooping down in order to do so. The angels desire thus to stoop down from the dizzy heights where they dwell to look into the great mysteries of our faith. There are at least five such marvels which fascinate those sinless sons of light.

First, the desire to look into <u>THAT CRADLE IN THE HAY</u>. Imagine what a stir there was on high when word was passed around that the Son of God was going down to planet earth to become the Son of man. One moment, heaven was ablaze with light. The next moment that light was shining on a cattle shed where a virgin was giving birth and a new star shone in the sky. Up in heaven they spread the news:

> *"Away in a manger, no crib for a bed,*
> *The little Lord Jesus lays down His sweet head;*
> *The star in the bright sky looked down where He lay;*
> *The little Lord Jesus asleep on the hay."*

This they must look into! And so they did! Down they came from the high halls of bliss and surrounded the nearby Judean hills desiring earnestly to look into what was transpiring on planet earth. And what do you think astonished them most? Nobody seemed to care. They raised their voices, they awoke the slumbering echoes of the hills and plains. "Unto you is born this day in the city of David," they cried, "a Savior which is Christ the Lord. Glory to God in the highest!" And nobody cared. A few shepherds looked timidly around, but that was all.

The angels ceased their songs. Then gazed in awe and wonder at the infant Christ, God's incarnate Son, their mighty Maker reduced to the size of a human babe, wrapped in baby clothes, cradled in a manger in a cattle shed. Back they went to Glory to proclaim the news on high.

Watch them as they arrive back on Heaven's shore. The other angels gather around. "And what of the sons of men?" they ask. "What of Adam's race? They must be thrilled to know that the captive planet earth has been invaded at last, and by no less a One than our Beloved. Fallen Lucifer's doom is sure. How did sinners take the news? By now the tidings must be heard in all Judea, in Jerusalem, in Athens and in Rome! There must be a stampede under way. Surely Herod has abdicated the throne by now. Surely Augustus must be bringing his legions to bow at His feet. The road to Bethlehem must be packed with people eager to look into these things."

"Interested? A stampede? No indeed! They couldn't care less. Indeed, there was no room for Him in the local inn so they gave Him a cattle barn in which to be born, a cave, no less, with manure on the floor for rugs, and cobwebs for drapes, and a food trough for His bed. Strange folk, these humans. How sad! How strong the stranglehold of sin!

And so it was. And so it is. The Son of God has come, and only a handful seem to care.

THINGS ANGELS DESIRE TO LOOK INTO (2)
I PETER 1:11-12

They looked into THE CRADLE IN THE HAY. That was something of consummate interest to them. That God should become a Man! Amazing! But that He should become a Man by such a process and for such a purpose and at such a place!

Thirty years of our time went by before we are told of the next thing that they desired to look into. Though doubtless no deed, no word, no choice of His failed to capture their interest. A thousand books could have been written about those silent, hidden years of His. To us, the activities of those thirty years are all unknown. But the angels watched and listened in awe—at the Babe, the Boy, the Teen, the Man—from the moment of His birth to the hour of His baptism at the hands of John.

Now comes the next turning point—THE CONFLICT IN THE WILDERNESS. The angels knew about sin and Satan because the whole great "mystery of iniquity" had all begun in heaven, not on earth. Moreover,

Lucifer appeared on high from time to time, summoned to appear before the throne of God to give account of his wanderings to and fro on the earth.

One member of the angelic order of the cherubim had done sentry duty at the gate of the garden of Eden right after the Fall. He was posted there to guard the way to the tree of life. So the Fall was a matter known on high. The interest of the angels was intensified by news that a fresh conflict was brewing. A second Man, a last Adam, was to take on fallen Lucifer. And under enormous handicaps. The Holy One would meet the Devil alone, in a waste, howling wilderness, after He had fasted right down to the very door of death, to a point where His physical resources were gone and His life hung by a thread. How different that scene to the glens and glades of Eden where the Fall of man had taken place.

Behind Jericho, in the deep depression of the Jordan, far below the level of the sea, there arose the Mount of Temptation. A climber would find that with every step up its slopes the scene became worse. The desolation that lay all around was that of a land accursed. The mountain itself was arid and naked. It was a mount of malediction. It rose in steep slopes from a sun-scorched plain and looked down on the sluggish waters of buried Sodom's sea. The Dead Sea, they called it; and a fitting name it was.

The battle began. It climaxed in the presentation of the same three temptations, though in different guise, which had conquered Eve and Adam himself—the lust of the flesh, the lust of the eye and the pride of life. The angels kept well back. This was no conflict of theirs. There must be no intrusion by them. But how they cheered when Satan, beaten again and again, finally fled from the scene. Then, and not till then, God sent one of the angels to visit the exhausted Conqueror.

The angel found his Lord at last, at the utter end of all endurance, physical, moral, spiritual. He lay there alone, exhausted, weak. But triumphant. Could this be? Was this He? It was. The Son of man, all victorious, crowned with glory and honor.

"Hello, Gabriel!" Surely some such word of welcome passed the Savior's lips. The angel, Gabriel or Michael or some unnamed member of the angel throng, ministered to Him. A drink of water from the crystal stream perhaps. A bed. A drawn sword to guard Him while He slept.

No doubt the other angels were full of questions when this privileged one arrived back home. "But were there no men there to care for Him? What about His friends, His family?" "No! There was no one. Only me."

So He fought that fight alone. And won! And Satan, skulking somewhere, in some haunted hollow, or in hiding behind Jupiter, perhaps, or Mars, knew that he had met his match at last. And he was terrified.

THINGS ANGELS DESIRE TO LOOK INTO (3)
I PETER.1:11-12

We have seen them looking into the cradle in the hay and into the conflict in the wilderness. Now we see them desiring to look into THE CLOISTER IN GETHSEMANE.

Just outside Jerusalem, on the lower slopes of Olivet, just across the Kidron, was a garden enclosed. It was a place of ancient trees. Their large twisted trunks and spreading branches, laden with fruit and foliage, formed a natural cloister, a retreat from the pressures of life. Jesus loved to go there. He could withdraw into its shadows and talk to His Father in heaven. It was called "Gethsemane"—The Oil Press. It was the last place the Lord sought out before He died. He came there to watch and weep and pray.

Mark tells us two things about the Lord's agony in that garden. First He withdrew from His three closest friends "a stone's cast." That phrase, "A stone's cast" has an ominous ring to it. The Jews executed criminals by stoning. So "a stone's cast" referred to the distance of death. For Jesus, death was not only a ston'e cast away.

Mark, doubtless conveying Peter's words says: "He (Christ) was "very heavy." The word he used means "deeply weighed down," or "depressed." Think of it! Jesus, the all-conquering Christ, He Who was always in control of every circumstance, depressed! In the upper room, just a short time ago, He had sung the Hebrew Hallelujah hymn. Now He groans, deeply weighed down by the thought of our sin.

Then, too, Mark tells us He was "greatly amazed," or "greatly astonished." The expression occurs only in Mark's gospel, and he uses it three times. He had used the word to describe the people at the foot of the Mount of Transfiguration when the Lord arrived in their midst, all aglow from His contact with heaven. He uses the word again, in connection with the appearance of the angel at the empty tomb of Christ. The word describes the reaction of the women. They were "affrighted," "thrown into terror." Now Mark uses the word to describe the Lord's grief in the garden. On both the other occasions (of the glow of Glory which still clung to Him as He came down from the mount, and of the shining one who guarded the tomb) the word is associated with another world. The same is true here. As He gazed into the dark and dreadful cup being presented to Him, He was overwhelmed by the world of evil He must now embrace. The old hymn catches the idea:

> "O Lord, what Thee tormented
> Was our sin's heavy load
> We had the debt augmented
> Which Thou must pay in blood."

The angels desired to look into all this. For this was beyond their understanding—their Beloved so identified with all the horror and wickedness of our sin as to actually "be made sin" for us.

And so it was, as He came close to death there in Gethsemane, at the thought of what lay ahead, angels came to strengthen Him. He must not die there, not there in a garden, but on a skull-shaped hill at a place called Calvary.

So the angels came. They ministered to Him and then, sadly, they went back home. And the heavenly hosts gather around again: "You say He was alone?" "Was there not a single one of Adam's race to wipe His brow and grip His hand?" "We saw three men not far off" the ministering angels would have replied, "They were friends of His—Peter, James and John He called them. But they were sound asleep."

So Peter, James and John missed it, the opportunity of a life time to minister to Him in His need. How often, one wonders, have we missed some similar occasion to win high recognition and eternal reward.

THINGS ANGELS DESIRE TO LOOK INTO (4)

I PETER 1:11-12

First it was <u>the cradle in the hay</u>. Then it was <u>the conflict in the wilderness</u>. Next it was <u>the cloister in Gethsemane</u>. Now it is <u>THE CRYPT IN THE GARDEN</u>. All these are things the angels have desired to look into. Twelve legions of warrior angels in high heaven, armed to the teeth, with drawn swords in their hands, strained over the battlements of heaven, watching these things. They were waiting for just one word from Him, that was all. They watched as men lied about their Beloved in their kangaroo court' as they blindfolded Him and punched Him in the face, as they crowned Him with thorns; as they ploughed His back like a farmer's field; as they proclaimed Him guiltless and then condemned Him to a felon's death; as they marched Him to a skull-shaped hill and spiked Him to a Roman tree. One word! That was all they wanted. It never came. Silently they put their swords away. Armageddon would have to wait. They stood around on high and watched Him take the scoffing and the scorn. They watched Him as He bowed His head and died.

Then came His friends. They took His torn and tattered body from the tree. Two men and a few sad women prepared His body for the tomb. Costly linens were produced and expensive ointments too. They wrapped Him around and around with bandages and fragrant spices. Then they put Him in a rich man's tomb in a garden in Jerusalem. They rolled a heavy stone in place and soldiers came and set the seal of Rome upon the sepulcher and left a guard to make sure no one tampered with that tomb.

The world spun on through space, carrying its priceless burden round and round its axis. Three long, dragging, endless days. Three dark, dreadful dreary nights. That incorruptible clay lay in that crypt dug into the rocky face of a Jerusalem hill. And, on high, the angels desired to look into these things.

Then it happened! The Lord returned from deep within the underworld, and entered the tomb unseen by the guard, and reentered His body, pure, untainted, untouched by the faintest indignity of decay. He shed the grave clothes, which by now were stiff as a plaster of Paris cast. He simply arose through them, then walked through the fast-sealed door and vanished.

Two of the angels came. Who were they? My guess would be Gabriel, the Messenger angel, communicator of God's will to men, and Michael, the martial angel, commander of the armies of heaven. With ineffable disdain for the soldiers, they broke the seal and rolled back the stone—not to let Christ out, not a bit of it! but to show that He was gone. Then they sat down and waited.

They thought, perhaps, that the Lord's disciples would remember His promise that on the third day He would rise again. Surely they would come with the morning light. A few women appeared and surely that stirred some interest. But, sudden disappointment, they had come to do some more burying! A couple of men came but did not stay. Nobody, it seemed to have believed a word that Jesus had said.

The angels went back home. We can picture the other angels crowding in. "Now surely," they would say, "surely the children of Adam came flocking to the tomb!" "No!" one of the two privileged angels would say. "No! In fact, one of the women who came seemed distraught. She turned her back on me and wrung her hands over the empty tomb. I overheard her talking to our Beloved as though He were some gardener fellow, and as though He had hidden the missing body somewhere." How stubborn is their unbelief! Yet our Lord loves them. He has great plans for them He says. These are some other things we should look into."

THINGS ANGELS DESIRE TO LOOK INTO (5)
I PETER 1:11-12

The cradle in the hay. The angels desired to look into that. The conflict in the wilderness, the cloister in Gethsemane, the crypt in the garden. These, too, they desired to probe. But there was something else, THE CONCEALMENT IN THE CLOUDS.

When God came down in olden times and pitched His tent among His people, He wrapped Himself around with a most unusual cloud. They called it "the Shekinah," the glory cloud. It sat upon the mercy seat upon the ark in the Holy of Holies. It spread out over the tents of the tribes so that the sun might not smite them by day nor the moon by night. Its presence was the visible token that God was in resident. It was His banner; and beneath its far-flung canopy, the saints could rest secure. It took the appearance of a pillar of cloud by day and of a pillar of fire by night. In Ezekiel's day, it had withdrawn itself because of the apostasy of the people. It had gone back to heaven and it had remained withdrawn throughout the remainder of the Old Testament era. Now the cloud was back, swirling and swaying above the Mount of Olives. The temple was ignored for its veil had been rent in two. God was no longer there. But the cloud was back. As the Savior made His way up Olivet, there it was, hovering on high, awaiting its Lord.

Forty days and forty nights had come and gone since His resurrection. Now He was going home, and the cloud awaited Him. The angels, too, were taking up their places in the sky. They had come to herald His birth, now they had come to welcome Him home.

It seems likely that all one hundred and twenty believers in the Lord were assembled on Olivet that day. They had marched with Him out of the city down and across the Kedron, past the Garden of Gethsemane, and on up to the top of the Mount. There the assembled band of believers halted. Pentecost was on its way. The Lord was going up and the Spirit was coming down. The Lord raised His hands in parting benediction. Then, silently and surely, He began to ascend. The astounded disciples stood there gazing up into heaven. Two of the angels detached themselves from His honor guard to come back with one last word. "He'll be back!" they said, "in this same way as He has gone!" Then they, too, were gone. For here was something they did not want to miss, something well worth looking into. They rejoined the angel escort, come to see Him home and to watch His investiture in heaven. As Son of man and Son of God, they saw Him sit down on the great white throne in heaven.

The angels still desire to look into these things. They are the talk of the ages up there. Yet, down here on earth, it is only with the greatest difficulty we can get anyone to listen when we talk of these things. Even those who say they love the Lord often pay but scant attention to these things. They neglect their Bibles, absent themselves from the meetings of the church, have little interest in spreading the Good News. The angels must surely look askance at all of us. To the angels, who desire earnestly to stoop down and look into these things, our indifference must seem like criminal neglect.

CALLED THE SONS OF GOD (1)
I JOHN 3

"Behold what manner of love the Father hath bestowed upon us that we should be called the sons of God." We can get into a family in three different ways. We can be <u>born</u> into a family, and in that case it is <u>life</u> that secures the relationship. We can be <u>adopted</u> into a family, in which case it is <u>law</u> that secures the relationship. Or we can be <u>married</u> into a family, in which case it is <u>love</u> that secures the relationship. The Christian is placed in the family of God in all three ways, Blessed be God! "A threefold cord cannot be broken (Ecc. 4:12)." The <u>Holy Spirit</u> is the One Who puts us in the family by birth. The <u>Father</u> is the One Who puts us in by adoption. The <u>Son</u> is the One Who puts us in by marriage. What more could we ask than that?

Now let us think what it means to have "such manner of love bestowed upon us that we should be called the sons of God." Let us picture ourselves in heaven as <u>the saints of all ages</u> go marching in to where Christ sits on the right hand of the majesty on high.

There goes Abel, the first martyr of the faith. And here comes Enoch, the first raptured saint of all time. Now it is the turn of Abraham, "the friend of God." Isaac follows, the man who was "obedient unto death." And there goes Jacob, now truly "a prince with God," and here comes Joseph, the most Christlike man in the Old Testament. And there is Job, of whom God said there was "none like him in the earth." And here comes Gideon, "mighty man of valor," that he was, and Samuel, last of the Old Testament judges and first of the Old Testament prophets. There goes Moses, the kinsman-redeemer of a nation, and

Daniel, "a man greatly beloved" and John the Baptist, called by Jesus "the greatest man born of a woman."

But wait! It's OUR TURN now. As we come to the reviewing stand, the high halls of heaven ring with applause. Everyone stands. The trumpet sounds. The herald angel announces our fame. "These are the sons of God! They are joint-heirs with Jesus Christ. They are seated with Him in the heavenlies, far above principalities and powers, thrones and dominions, and every name which is named, not only in this world but also in the world to come." Such is the manner of love the Father hath bestowed upon us.

"Therefore the world knoweth us not," John adds, "because it knew Him not."

Look what the world did to God's beloved Son. He came down here and lived on earth for thirty-three years. "He went about doing good," Peter says. He lived His whole life in the service of our fellow race. He healed the sick and raised the dead. He made the blind to see and the deaf to hear. He cleansed lepers and cast out evil spirits. He changed water into wine and fed the hungry multitudes. He loved His enemies and died to save them. He taught the sublimest truths in the simplest of terms. He was love incarnate. And this world crucified Him.

If they knew Him not, it is no wonder they know us not, John says.

But the Father knows us! And He is on the throne. We may be despised and rejected of men down here, but we are assured of a tumultuous welcome when we arrive up there. Once we get over Jordan, the Promised Land awaits and the Father's welcoming smile and high seats in heaven itself.

LOVE THE FATHER HATH BESTOWED (2)

I JOHN 3:1

When John wrote his first epistle, apostasy had already taken deep root in the church. The up and coming heresy was gnosticism. It denied the truth along three lines. The Ebionites denied the Deity of Christ. According to them, He was just another created being. The Docetists denied the humanity of Christ. They said He was some kind of a phantom, void of physical being and denied He had come in the flesh. The followers of <u>Cerinthus</u> denied the union of the two natures of Christ, the human and the Divine, prior to His baptism. An entity they called "The Christ" supposedly descended on Jesus at His baptism and abandoned Him prior to His crucifixion. It was all what J. B. Phillips calls "intellectualism and high-sounding nonsense" (Col. 2:8).

If anyone knew the truth about Christ, it was John. He knew the truth, for instance, about the Lord's mother. He had been Mary's protector after the crucifixion, confided to his care by Jesus Himself. John knew perfectly well that neither Joseph or anyone else was the father of Jesus.

As for His Deity, there was plenty of evidence for that. He had turned water into wine, and fed the hungry multitudes with a little lad's lunch. He had walked upon the waves and stilled a raging storm. The world itself could not contain the books which could have been written about Him, John said (John 21:25). He had healed the sick, cleansed lepers, raised the dead and conquered the tomb. John, now an old man, had been an eyewitness of these things. His scornful answer to Gnostic nonsense was simple, but adequate: "<u>I was there</u>!"

Jesus was God. He was Man. He was both. He was God, in every sense of the word, possessed of all the attributes of Deity. He was Man, perfectly human with a human body and mind and emotions and will. He fell asleep in Peter's boat—that was His humanity. Moments later He commanded wind and waves to be still—that was His Deity. He asked a woman at a well for a drink because He was thirsty. That was His humanity. Then He told her all about her life. That was His Deity. It is impossible to say where the one ends and the other begins.

Against this background, John brought his readers back to basics: "Behold what manner of love the Father hath bestowed upon us that we should be called the Sons of God. . . ." What manner of love indeed!

"Father!" That in itself was different. The Old Testament had revealed God as Elohim and as Jehovah, as Adonai and as God Most High, as Jehovah-jireh and as El-Shaddai. Jesus revealed Him as "Our Father which art in heaven."

Some years ago, a book was published entitled, "Letters from Hell. The Correspondence of A Lost Soul." "Was there not something in vanished time," the lost one asks, "something called 'The Lord's Prayer,' beginning with 'Our Father . . . ? I vainly try to recall the sacred words. I set out to say the prayer but never get beyond 'Our Father.' I repeat these words fifty times but never get beyond 'Our Father.' I just remember there <u>is</u> a Father, but He is not my Father. And I am not His child. I keep on saying the two words. My soul is thirsting for their comfort. But I can find no drop of water to cool my tongue."

What a tragedy! To know that God's manner of love would gladly put is in His family, now and forever but to end up refusing to let Him do so. For we must be willing to have Him be our Father. He invites us but never compels.

WHAT MANNER OF LOVE (3)
I CORINTHIANS 13/I JOHN 3:1-3

LOVE THAT IS SOVEREIGNLY BESTOWED

We are invited to consider "what <u>manner</u> of love" it is that God bestows upon us. "God is love," we read (a John 4:8). "God is light," we also read (1 John 1:5). The one Divine attribute illustrates the other. Take light, for instance. Pass it through a prism, and it breaks up into seven colors. Pass sunlight through the storm, and it will produce a rainbow. Take the seven colors of the spectrum, and put them in motion; and they will merge into one—the color of light.

Just as there are seven colors which comprise light, so there are nine components which comprise love. Paul describes them in 1 Corinthians 13. They are—patience, kindness, generosity, humility, courtesy, unselfishness, good temper, guilessness and sincerity.

Take the nine components of love, and put them in motion; and they all merge into the essence of what God is: <u>God is love</u>. God proposes to bestow His love, in all its completeness and according to its various components, on us. <u>That</u> is "the manner of love" God sovereignly bestows. It expresses itself uniquely thus: "<u>That we should be called the sons of God.</u>" We! We who were sinners of Adams' ruined race are now <u>sons of God</u>. The hymnwriter puts it like this:

"Great God of wonders, all Thy ways
Display Thine attributes Divine,
But the rich glories of Thy grace
Above Thine other wonders shine."

God is omnipotent, of course! God is omniscient, it goes without saying! God is omnipresent, that is so. But here is the supreme wonder: <u>God is love</u>. However, that is not just an attribute, it is the ultimate face of His being. He bestows this love sovereignly on us, calling us "<u>Sons</u> of God.

LOVE THAT IS SWEETLY CONFIRMED

"Behold now <u>are</u> we the sons of God." Blessed be God our God! That means that we, too, are to shed love abroad in this dark world of sin.

Henry Drummond once said: "In the heart of Africa, among the great lakes, I have come across black men and women who remembered the only white man they ever saw—David Livingstone, and as you cross his footsteps in that dark continent, men's faces light up as they speak of the kind doctor who passed there three years ago. "Behold, now are we the sons of God."

LOVE THAT IS SUDDENLY COMPLETE

"It doth not yet appear what we shall be, but we know that when He shall appear we shall be like Him for we shall see Him as He is!" Theologians talk of perfect sanctification and progressive sanctification. The moment we are saved we are made perfect in Christ. "For He hath made Him to be sin for us, Who knew no sin; that we might be made the righteousness of God in Him" (2 Cor. 5:21). God sees us robed in the righteousness of Christ. We are as fit for heaven as though we were already there. We have perfect sanctification. God looks at us in Christ and sees Him. That is perfect sanctification.

However, we are still in the body, and have to do daily battle with the flesh. Our standing is perfect, our state is not. The indwelling Holy Spirit works with our human spirit to produce the fruit of the Spirit. We are to be progressively fruitful in every good work, increasing in the knowledge of God (Col.1:10).

But one of these days He Himself will appear. We shall see Him as He is. Instantly we shall be like Him. That perfect sanctification, which now is only reckoned to us (Rom.6:7, 11-13), will be realized by us.

The old chorus only expresses our longing:

"Be like Jesus, this my song,
In the home and in the throng;
Be like Jesus all day long,
I would be like Jesus."

When we see Him as He is, the transformation will take place. We shall be like Jesus indeed.

WHY? BUT!
PSALM 22:1-6

Psalm 22 was written by David a thousand years before the birth of Christ. It contains no less than thirty-three distinct prophecies which were all literally fulfilled at Calvary. Who, but God, could so foretell the future? This psalm, for instance, records Emmanuel's orphan cry, that great cry of desolation which rang during the midday-midnight darkness which wrapped Him around in His agony on the cross.

We know that David was the human author of this psalm; but that only deepens the mystery because, though David knew what was to suffer, he never even so much as approximated the sufferings described here. The Holy Spirit simply took what could only have been hyperbole in David's case, and transformed it into prophecy when David wrote it down.

The suffering Savior felt Himself abandoned by both God and man. We note the great gulf fixed which separated Him from AN ALL-HOLY GOD (1-3). "My God! My God! Why hast Thou forsaken Me?" He added, "Why art Thou so far from helping Me and from the words of My roaring?" The Hebrew word for "roaring" is used for the roar of a lion and also for the cry of an animal in pain.

"Why? Why?" He cried, but there was no answer. Then the suffering Savior changed the word "why" for the word "but." He said, "But Thou Art holy!" That was it! The amazing and awesome mystery is that He had been made sin for us. He did not become sinful, perish the thought! He became <u>sin</u> and "tasted death." A whole eternity was sandwiched into that dreadful period of time on the cross which began with the sixth hour and ended with the ninth hour. During that period total darkness held the whole land in its grip and Jesus experienced the ultimate terror of the lost, the horror of being left, in the dark, abandoned by God.

There was also the great gulf fixed which separated Him from ALL HOLY MEN (4-6). Others cried and were heard. Abraham cried! Moses cried! David cried! God heard them. Jesus cried, and there was no reply.

Again the suffering Savior found a use for that little word "but." "But," He said, "I am a worm and no man." Who can plumb the depths of <u>that</u>? We could have understood it had He said He was a lion, or a lamb. But a <u>worm</u>? We count a worm as being very low indeed in our scale of things. We forget that, in God's sovereign dealings with Jonah, the worm was as necessary as the wind and the whale. Just the same, we don't think much of worms! That is why we are so startled to hear the Savior say: "I am a worm."

The Lord, however, did not use the word for an ordinary worm. On the contrary, He made reference to the crimson crocus, which, when crushed, yielded the scarlet dye. It was a fitting type of the stricken Christ, Who we see on Calvary, "dying, crushed beneath the lead of the wrath and curse of God." Well might the hymnwriter say:

> *"O make me understand it*
> *Help me to take it in;*
> *What it meant for Thee, the Holy One*
> *To take away my sin."*

As He Is

I John 4:17

"As He is, so are we, in this world." What could be <u>simpler</u> than that? Nine words, all of one syllable, and six of them with only two letters—"As He is, so are we, in this world." Yet, what could be <u>sublimer</u> than that? The text is so complex it is hard to know where to begin. Let us begin with Him.

We note, first, THE PLAN. We are to be like Him. But that is not quite so simple as it sounds. We are reminded of the little black boy who over simplified his situation. A man asked him his name. He said, "My name is George Washington." The man said, "Well, if your name is George Washington, you'd better make sure you behave like George Washington." "Ah can't help but live like George Washington," the boy replied. "Ah is George Washington".

"As He is!" When we think of Him as He is, we realize, of course, that He is not as He was. He is living a transformed life. Up until about two thousand years ago, He lived an eternal life, as the uncreated, self-existing Son of the living God, invisible and infinite. Then something happened. He was born! He became a man, and in Him, now, and forever, "dwells all the fullness of the Godhead bodily" (Col.2:9).

Moreover, He lives a triumphant life. He is God manifest in flesh. In His life down here on earth He triumphed over sin, over Satan and over situations. As a Babe and as a Boy, at home and at play, in the school and in the synagogue, as the village carpenter and as the miracle-working Christ, He lived in triumph. Not once, in thought or word or deed, did He deviate from the path of obedience to His Father in heaven. His foes tried to get rid of Him by putting Him to death, but He rose a victor from the dark domain. Now He was ascended and sits, in a human, though resurrected, body as God over all, blessed for evermore, on the throne of His Father in heaven.

Now comes THE PLEDGE—"As He is, so are we." We, too, have experienced a change. We, too, live a transformed life. We have been born again. At the time of our conversion, the Holy Spirit indwelt our body and our being. We are now inhabited by God for our human spirit has been quickened by God's Holy Spirit. As He became flesh and dwelt among us, as God manifest in flesh, so now we have become people indwelt by God.

Which means that we now are to live a triumphant life, victorious over sin, Satan and situations. Our life is a continuation of His life, made possible by the indwelling, filling and anointing of the Holy Spirit. The use of the formula "as. . . . even so" in the Bible always depict an exact similarity.

Finally, mention is made of THE PLACE. All are ready to agree that we are to be like Him in heaven. John himself says as much: "We shall be like Him for we shall see Him as He is." But note this: "As He is, so are we in this world." Not only then and there, but also here and now.

A Christian lady saw a shoeless boy gazing longingly at shoes in a shop window. Touched, she took him in and bought him some shoes and socks, washed his feet and put them on him. "Please, ma'am," said the little boy, "are you Christ's wife?"

As He is, so are we in this world. As the chorus puts it:
"Be like Jesus this my song,
In the home and in the throng.
Be like Jesus all day long,
I would be like Jesus."

ALL ARE YOURS

I Corinthians 3:21-23

Some years ago the wife of a friend of mine lay dying from a particularly painful kind of cancer. My friend loved his wife dearly. The thought of her dying wracked his very soul. The sight of her dying in agony drove him to distraction.

Then the emissaries of a religious group assured him that, if he had enough faith, his wife would be healed. When I went to see him, he was pacing the corridors of the hospital, convinced that his lack of faith was the reason she was still slowly, painfully dying in her bed. This cruel "teaching" had just about finished him. I took him down to the coffee shop and sought to comfort him. I turned in my Bible to 1 Corinthians 3:21-23.

"Now, Claude," I said, "look at some of the things the Holy Spirit says are yours—Paul, Apollos, the world, life death, things present, things to come. These four things are yours, given to you by a Sovereign God, One Who controls all the factors of time, matter and space.

"NO MATTER WHO (Whether Paul, or Apollos or Cephas). These men represent true apostles and true Bible teachers. We are to listen to such as these, giving honor where honor is due, avoiding false apostles and false prophets. We listen to those truly called, gifted and anointed of God, thankful for any measure of truth they have to impart.

NO MATTER WHERE ("the world"). It makes no difference to the Lord whether we are in this town or that one, this hospital or some other He rules the world.

NO MATTER WHAT ("Life or death"). Jesus is the life and He has conquered death and holds it key.

NO MATTER WHEN ("Things present or things to come"). Jesus transcends all time. He has conquered time. He inhabits eternity. The past, the present and the future are all the same to Him.

"Now notice," I said, "that God has given all these things to you. All of them, in their own proper time and place, are yours. Right now one of these is especially yours—death! God has given death to you as His gift. That may sound strange but think what it means.

"Mary is going to die because her condition is terminal. The though troubles you, it torments you. But it is so. She is going to die. You must not blame yourself and torture yourself on that account. Her death is not your fault. No, indeed! God is now giving you death as His kind and living gift. He is too loving to be unkind. He is too wise to make any mistakes. He is too powerful to be hindered. Death is about release your beloved from her suffering and pain. It is soon to open for her the gates of glory. It will lift her into that land where they count not time by years, to where Christ sits at the right hand of God. She will be absent from that pain-wracked body of hers, and she will be present with the Lord. All this death will do for her and you. She will cease to suffer. She will be at rest, safe in the arms of Jesus. And you will be able to rest in the certain knowledge that she is with the Lord. Then time ("things to come") another of God's gifts to you, will heal your hurts as well."

The lines of anguish slowly faded from his face. "Thank you," he said, "I needed that."

CALVARY AND THE OFFERINGS
LUKE 24:25-27

At 6:00 AM the BURNT OFFERING was offered.[1] The burnt offering was all for God. It was an offering which depicted Jesus as One Who was "obedient unto death, even the death of the cross." The sacrifice to be declared perfect, without spot or blemish. The exploring knife opened up the inward parts for inspection. The devouring flame caused the sweet-smelling savor of the sacrifice to ascend to God. It was about this time that Jesus stood before Pilate who pronounced Him sinless: "I find no fault in this man at all," he declared.

At 9:00 AM the MEAL OFFERING was offered. The meal offering was of fine flour, ground until it was free from unevenness. It was then mixed with oil. It represents the perfect life of Christ energized by the Holy Spirit. There was no leaven in the meal offering (leaven is always a symbol of sin) and no honey (a symbol of mere natural sweetness) to be added to this offering. No energy of the flesh was even present in the life of the Lord Jesus. All was energized by the Spirit of God. The meal offering is described as "an offering of the Lord made by fire." It points to Christ Who, having been declared faultless by Pilate, was handed over to him to suffering and to death.

At 12:00 noon the PEACE OFFERING was offered. By that time, the Lord Jesus had been on the cross for three hours. At twelve noon the darkness came down upon the scene as the Lord Jesus "made peace by the blood of His cross" (Col.1:20) He was "made sin" (2 Cor. 5:21) for us so that sin which God hates might be dealt with once and for all. Peace means that the war is over. The peace offering brought God and man together around the table. It became the foundation of a feast—but at uttermost cost to the ox or the lamb that was offered. Thus our Lord, Who endured the cross despising the shame, now ensures our peace with God and brings us into His banqueting house where His banner over us is love.

At 3:30 PM the SIN OFFERING was offered, the offering which dealt with the principle of sin. "I am not a sinner because I sin; I sin because I am a sinner", just as an apple tree is not an apple tree because it bears apples; it bears apples because it is an apple tree. We do what we do because we are what we are. The sin offering was designed to deal with our sin nature. At 3:00 PM Jesus said, "It is finished." The work was done. Atonement had been made. Sin's awful price was paid in full.

At 6:00 the TRESPASS OFFERING was offered. The trespass offering dealt with the <u>practice</u> of sin, with sin against one's fellow man. The sin offering dealt with our sin; the trespass offering deals with our sins. By 6:00 PM, the time when the trespass offering was sacrificed the sufferings of Christ were all over. The Lord Jesus was already in the tomb of his fellow man.

The law of the trespass offering required that full restoration be made to the one who had been robbed. More, an additional twenty percent had to be added so the robbed became the gainer. The Lord arose from that borrowed tomb of his, and both God in heaven and the believer on earth become gainers. God became a gainer because Calvary had provided Him with an adequate stage upon which He could demonstrate His love. God's wisdom and His power are adequately displayed in creation; His love is seen in our redemption.

Man has become a gainer, too, because of Calvary. Adam, we may suppose, could have remained in Eden for a million years and then have fallen into sin, and died. The salvation Jesus procured for us places us forever beyond the reach of sin and death forever. If, on the other hand, neither Adam nor his posterity had ever sinned, his offspring would continue to be children of Adam, nothing more. By virtue of Calvary we become children of God and joint heirs with Jesus Christ. Moreover, we are seated in the heavenlies, exalted on high. All this lay latent in symbolic teaching of that final offering of the day.

---

[1] I am indebted to Ed Vallowe, a preacher friend of mine, and one of the best informed students of the Word I know, for the information here regarding the timing of the daily sacrifices.

THE COLT

EXODUS 34:20; LUKE 19:28-40

The lowly donkey is mentioned over a hundred and forty times in Scripture. The first mention is in connection with Abraham who, when told by God to go to Mount Moriah, there to offer up his well-beloved son, immediately saddled his ass and prepared for the journey. Then there was the Good Samaritan's donkey, and what about Balaam's ass which rebuked the madness of the prophet? But surely the donkey which heads the list is this one, mentioned in the Gospels, the one which helped the Lord Jesus fulfill an ancient prophecy (Zech.9:9).

There are three things worth noting about this donkey. First, IT HAD TO BE REDEEMED. The law of Moses pronounced the donkey an unclean animal. Id did not chew the cud, and it did not have a cloven hoof; so it was doubly cursed. Inside and out, it was declared to be unclean; and the law demanded that any firstborn ass should be put to death. But the law also made provision for the condemned beast, it could be redeemed. A lamb could die in its stead. It could live because a substitute had taken its place and died.

The application is to us. We are born unclean, condemned by God's law and sentenced to death. A Lamb (the Lord Jesus) has died so that we might go free. For, like that donkey of old, we needed to be redeemed. How grateful we should be to the Lord of Glory Who took our place and died that we might live. Truly we now live the life of Another, even of Him Who interposed His precious blood and paid our debt and gave us His life.

But this colt needed not only to be redeemed, IT HAD TO BE RELEASED: "Ye shall find a colt tied, whereon never man sat," Jesus told His disciples, "loose him, and bring him here." It had life, thanks to the lamb, but it did not have liberty. That colt may have stood alongside the post to which it was tied and dreamed about being set free. The grass on the hills looked so green. The brook down the hill looked so refreshing. The other animals seemed to be roaming at will. But he was tied to a post. It was set free by the Word of Christ and by means of His authority.

Again, the application is to us. Many have new life in Christ but are still in bondage to old habits and sins. They need to hear the Word of the Lord: "Loose him! Bring him to Me." How grateful that little colt must have been when the Lord's disciples undid the knots which bound him to that post. He kicked up his heels. He was free.

But there was something else. IT HAD TO BE RULED. This was a colt "upon which yet never man set." It was an unbroken colt, full of the pride of life and self-will. But the Lord had not set it free to please itself, but to serve Him. "Bring him to Me," He said.

Then a wonderful thing happened. The Master enthroned Himself upon him as Lord of its life. All rebellion fled. All fear vanished. The colt was transformed from a wild, untamed creature to an obedient, submissive instrument of the Master's will. Its one duty now was to lift up the Lord Jesus. And so it did. As a result the people saw Christ and shouted his praise. All eyes were on Jesus, not on the Donkey; and that, of course, is the way it ought to be.

> *"How I praise Thee precious Savior*
> *That Thy love laid hold of me,*
> *Thou hast saved and cleansed and filled me*
> *That I might Thy channel be."*

WHO?

ROMANS 8:32F

God throws down the gauntlet to all the enemies of His people. "Who?" He says, "Who shall lay anything to the charge of God's elect?" Satan comes, eager to take up the challenge. He comes as the ACCUSER. He is the ancient father of lies, well versed in the art of deceit. The great idiom of his language is the lie. "Tell a lie big enough, often enough, and people will believe it," is his philosophy. However, when he comes into the presence of God, He does not come to tell lies. No lie can last a moment in the burning light in which God dwells. Moreover, sad to say, Satan has no need to tell lies, when he comes into the presence of God to tell tales about us. He needs only to tell the truth about us. So he takes up the challenge. "Who shall lay anything to the charge of God's elect?" "I will," he says, "as the Accuser of the brethren."

God throws down the gauntlet again. "Who?" He says, "Who shall separate us from the love of God?" It is love as vast, as deep and as wide as eternity. Satan comes again, this time as the ADVERSARY. He has a thousand means at his command to torment, torture and terrify that "feeble folk," as he sees them, who make up the ranks of the people of God.

But Satan does not have a chance. For be he Accuser or Adversary (Devil or Satan), he is confronted at once by the ADVOCATE (1 Jno. 2:1).

"So," says our Advocate with the Father, "You are the Accuser, are you? Well, lay your charge." But even as he begins the sad tale of all the sins and shortcomings of even the saintliest of the people of God, he is put to silence. "You are talking of those whom God Himself has justified," The Advocate declares. He shows His hands still bearing the marks of Calvary where the sin question was settled once and for all. "There are no such sins as those you mention. In fact, there are no sins at all. God remembers them no more" (Heb. 8:12; 10:17).

Satan tries again. "So," says our Advocate, "you have come back, have you? You are here now as the Adversary. You want to separate God's people from God's love. Impossible! What weapons do you have?"

"What about the inevitable? What about "death or life?" Death is no use to you because I have the keys of death. Life offers you no advantage. I am the Life."

"What about the invisible? What about "angels, principalities and powers?" At Calvary I made an open show of the likes of those" (Col.2:15).

"What about the inescapable? What about "things present or things to come?" I am the great I AM, the ever-present One; and I am the coming One. Nothing you have, now or then, will be of use to you."

"What about the incalculable? What about "height or depth?" I have been down to the deepest depths. I reign in the highest heights. You have no hope or advantage there.

"What about the inconceivable? What about "any other creature?" I am the Creator. "There is no created being in the whole wide universe over which I do not exercise absolute power. As for you, you have no power. Nothing can separate mine from Me. Satan, you are a defeated foe." And so He is!

Hallelujah! What a Savior!

The Four Faces Of Self
Romans 6-7

By the time Paul arrived at Romans 6, he had the answer to the sovereignty of self in the soul of a saint. He tells us we are not free to sin, we are free from sin. We who once were dead in sin are now dead to sin. The Lord of Glory Who gave His life for us now lives, in the power of resurrection, to give His life to us. It is a matter of the right use of the humble preposition.

That is very good news indeed. It is such good news that Paul presents it to us in four unforgettable illustrations. He tells us, first, that the old nature in the believer is like AN OLD MAN, a wicked old man. Scofield renders Paul's expression, "the old man," more vividly as "the man of old," the man we used to be. We are born with a fallen nature, a nature which can do nothing right. We are born again with a Divine nature, a nature that can do nothing wrong. The two natures are at war. But here is God's answer to "the old man" and his deeds. The old man is now dead, he says. He is "crucified with Christ."

We find it hard to believe such an awesome truth because the old nature doesn't feel dead. Feelings, however, do not alter facts. God says that the old nature is dead; and the whole machinery of redemption operates on the assumption that God says what He means, and means what He says. We must take God at His word in all this.

Next, the old nature in the believer is like AN OLD MONARCH. God gave dominion over everything to Adam but, when tempted, Adam surrendered his sovereignty to Satan. As a result, we were born into a world controlled by the Evil one. We were born subject to sin, self and Satan. The old monarch, however, is now defeated. At Calvary the Lord Jesus triumphed gloriously over Satan and despoiled principalities and powers. Every believer is automatically constituted a citizen of the kingdom of God. "Let not sin therefore reign," Paul says. "Sin shall not have dominion over you," he adds. We must take God at His word.

Then, too, the old nature is like AN OLD MASTER. We were born slaves to sin, a bondage into which we were sold by Adam. We have inherited his fallen, sinful nature. We know by bitter experience the bondage of

62

evil habits. Two thousand years ago, however, the Lord Jesus came into the slave market of sin and paid the price of our redemption. He purchased, at infinite cost, with His own blood, and has set us free. So, the old master is now desposed. We no longer need to obey its wicked demands. "Being made free from sin," says Paul, "ye became the servants of righteousness," servants of God no less.

Finally, the old nature is likened to AN OLD MARRIAGE. When Adam fell, the whole human race was potentially in him. As a result, all his posterity are born married, as it were, to sin, and what a hideous and hateful marriage it is! We live on the most intimate terms with sin. We go to bed with it at night. We get up with it in the morning. We live with it moment by moment throughout the day. Consciously, or carelessly we live as those who are married to sin. But this old marriage is now dissolved. Not only did our death with Christ put an end to the old marriage, we are now "married to Another, even to Him Who is raised from the dead." Now we live in intimacy with that glorious Man Who reigns on high and, in consequence of this intimacy, bring forth fruit unto God. An old man, now dead! An old monarch, now defeated! An old master, now desposed! An old marriage now dissolved! What more could we want than that?

WITNESSES UNTO ME
ACTS 1:8

For a period of forty days, between First fruits and Pentecost, the risen Lord tarried here on earth. Over yonder the standards of the Almighty were unfurled. To the utmost bounds of the everlasting hills, the heralds had borne the news: "The Lord is risen indeed." The morning stars sang together, and all the sons of God shouted for joy. Twelve legions of angels were drawn up in battle array along the jasper battlements of heaven and at the gates of pearl. Eager eyes were watching. But still he did not come. Still He tarried, even though His own heart was hungry for home. He stayed because He had one more thing to do—prepare the disciples for the task He had in mind.

First, they needed ENLISTMENT, so He made His <u>passion</u> known to them. He wanted them to reach "the uttermost parts of the earth." They were to witness to Him in Jerusalem, in Judea, in Samaria, and to earth's remotest bounds. They were to meet a man from Ethiopia and a man from Macedonia. They were to meet men and women, boys and girls from all parts of the world. It was to be the whole duty of the whole church for the whole age. That was His passion. The whole world must know the good news that Christ died for their sins, that He was buried and that He rose again.

Moreover, they needed ENCOURAGEMENT, so He made His <u>presence</u> known to them. He Himself would be with them, always, and to the end of the world. So He showed Himself alive, after His passion, "by many infallible proofs." The task was thus simplified. They were not called to preach a dogma or a creed or found a new religion. They were called to preach Christ, to tell people of a living, relevant Person. They were to make Him real to other people. However, before we can make Him real to anyone else, He has to be real to us. So the Lord appeared here, He showed up there. He made Himself real to this one and to that one. They needed to become convinced of His abiding presence, that He was there, alongside them, whether seen or unseen. He was there as He promised and would be to the end of time (Matt.28:19-20). He appeared to each in a different way. With Mary, it was the whisper of her name. With the Emmaus disciples, it was the exposition of the Word. With Thomas it was his hands and feet and side. By the time He was through, they were all convinced of the reality of His resurrection, His rapture and His return.

Then, too, they needed ENLIGHTENMENT, so He made His <u>program</u> known to them. They were to begin in their own community, Jerusalem. They were to reach their own country, Judea. They were to evangelize their own continent, beginning with Samaria, the closest alien culture. They were to reach the whole, wide world. That was the plan. The book of Acts shows how closely and how successfully that plan was followed.

Finally, they needed ENABLEMENT, so He made His <u>power</u> known to them. For He had set before them the impossible task of persuading people to repent of their sins, to turn to Christ, to accept Him by faith, and have their lives transformed. The problem was they were powerless to witness. When Mary Magdalene, Joanna, Mary the mother of Jesus and other women told the Twelve that Jesus was alive, "their words seemed to them

64

as idle tales, and they believed them not." When the Emmaus disciples arrived back in Jerusalem with the news of a risen Christ, "neither believed they them." When all ten of them tried to convince Thomas, he said, "I will not believe." They needed enablement.

"Ye shall receive power," Jesus said. "After the Holy Ghost is come upon you." And so they did! For it is only the Holy Spirit Who can make Christ real to an unregenerate and disbelieving heart. And that is exactly what He did on the day of Pentecost, and with such phenomenal success that thousands were swept into the kingdom of heaven that very same day.

As . . .

I PETER

Peter had learned from Jesus how to paint pictures with words, how to use figures of speech. He specializes in the strategic use of similes. For example, he says that we were AS SHEEP GOING ASTRAY (2:25). It is astonishing how often the Bible likens people to animals, to wolves and dogs and sows. Jesus called Herod a fox. He likened Himself to a hen. We are all likened to sheep.

A sheep is not strong, and it is not swift, and it is not smart. It has a tendency to stray and put itself in peril. Moreover, a sheep that strays soon finds itself lost and with no ability to find its way back to the fold. Peter said that we, wayward sheep that we are, have "now returned." A sheep can only be returned to the shepherd if the shepherd seeks and finds it. That, then, is what happened, and what rejoicing that causes in heaven. As the hymnwriter puts it:

> *"Up through the mountain thunder riven*
> *And up from the rocky steep*
> *There arose a cry to the gate of heaven*
> *'Rejoice I have found my sheep!'*
> *And the angels echoed around the throne*
> *'Rejoice for the Lord brings back His own.'"*

We were AS NEWBORN BABES (2:2). The one characteristic of a newborn babe is its utter helplessness and obvious need. Therefore a local church is to be an incubator, not a refrigerator. Some churches are so cold, it is no wonder they see no one saved. They remind us of the little girl who learned a text in Sunday School: "Many are called but few are chosen." When asked to recite it, she said: "Many are cold and a few are frozen!" New converts need love and care; and when they get themselves in a mess, they need to be cleaned up. They need to be fed. We cannot expect babes in Christ to act like mature saints of God. We need to feed them "the sincere milk of the Word" so that they will grow in grace and increase in the knowledge of God.

We are AS OBEDIENT CHILDREN (2:14). Peter contrasts "the former lusts" with "the family likeness." Babes in Christ must be taught obedience to the Word of God. The Lord Jesus Himself "learned obedience" (Heb.5:8) and became "obedient unto death" (Phil.2:8). Peter says: "Be ye holy for I am holy," saith the Lord. This Old Testament quotation is appended to a chapter which lists all the dietary "do's" and "don'ts" of the Law (Lev.11). There is always the danger of thinking that we have discharged our religious obligations when we have conformed with some rule or ritual. God demands much more than that. He demands holiness.

Moreover, we are AS STRANGERS AND PILGRIMS (2:11). Cain described himself as a fugitive and a vagabond. By contrast, Abraham confessed himself to be a pilgrim and a stranger. The sons of Heth, however, said he was a mighty prince among them. Nobody ever said that of Lot who gave up being a pilgrim and a stranger in order to get on in this world. A stranger is a man away from home. He is an alien and out of his environment. His looks, his language and his likings are all different from those round about him. He is a citizen of another country. A pilgrim is more than a man away from home, he is going home. He has his mind set on a long-desired place. Our affections are to be set thus on things above where Christ sits at the right hand of the Majesty on high. We're going home.

Finally, we are AS LIVING STONES (2:5). The Lord once called Peter a pebble petros, and Himself a Rock Petra (Matt. 16:18). Peter carries the simile over the all believers. We are to be living stones, hewed out of nature's dark mine, shaped and fashioned by the Holy Spirit and fitted by God into that "habitation of God through the Spirit" He is now erecting for eternity. When David Livingstone went to Africa, it was to evangelize, to explore and to emancipate. When He died, a grieving nation followed his coffin to Westminster Abbey where he was buried along with many of England's great. One of the nation's most popular periodicals wrote his epitaph. It read: "Granite may crumble but this is living stone." Well may we strive so that some such epitaph might one day be ours.

Inside Out

Two truths were at the heart of all the activity which took place on the Day of Atonement. Predominantly the High Priest was occupied with two goats. The blood of one he took <u>inside</u>, inside the veil, there to sprinkle it on and before the Mercy Seat. The other goat became the sin-bearer and was handed over to a fit man to be taken <u>outside</u> the camp. Jesus, our Great High Priest, suffered <u>outside</u>. He was crucified outside the city of Jerusalem and outside the camp of Israel. Now He is seated <u>inside</u>, inside the veil on the very throne of God in heaven.

First, HE CAME FROM THE INSIDE TO THE OUTSIDE. He stepped out of eternity into time, "out of the ivory palaces, into a world of woe." He came from the innermost sanctuary of Glory, from the Holy Mount and from the midst of the stones of fire to enter into human life on a rebel planet in space. The people on this planet killed Him outside the camp, on a skull-shaped hill outside the city walls. Then, as a final act of rejection, they sealed Him in a tomb. They could thrust Him out no further. That was it.

But HE RETURNED FROM THE OUTSIDE TO THE INSIDE. Death could not hold Him. They slammed shut the door of His tomb and set the official seal upon it, but they could not lock Him in that dark, cold grave. He arose! He went where He willed, did as He liked and there was no one to stop Him. Not all the military might of Rome could hinder Him in His comings and goings, here and there, hither and yon. After forty days, He went back home to heaven. In He went, in through the gates into Glory. Back He went to the throne. Now His back is on the <u>inside</u> once more.

67

Soon HE WILL COME BACK FROM THE INSIDE TO THE OUT-SIDE. One of these days He will descend from heaven with a shout! He will sweep across the world like a storm, faster than the lightning, swifter than the wind. He will empty the graves of all the believing dead and snatch away all living children of God and unbelievers will not even know He has come and gone again. Still less will they mobilize any opposition. For this will be just a flying visit to a rebel planet on the outside of things. It will be a visit like the visit of a thief in the night. It will be a flying visit to the outside to receive to Himself His own.

Then HE WILL TAKE US WITH HIM FROM THE OUTSIDE TO THE INSIDE. Up we will go! In we will go! In through the wide-flung gates of Glory. Millions of people will be with Him marching down the golden highway, into the inner sanctuary on high. Right up to His Father's throne we will go. There He will present us faultless while the hosts of heaven applaud and sing. We shall be on the inside indeed!

Finally HE WILL BRING US FROM THE INSIDE TO THE OUT-SIDE. For on earth, things will have gone from woe to woe. By the time we will have appeared at the Judgment Seat of Christ and all spots and blemishes been forever removed things will be reaching their final crescendo of horror and despair down here. The maddened and desperate multitudes will be massed by the million at Megeddo. The last war is about to begin. Who is to rule the world? east or west? That is what the Battle of Armageddon is all about. But before that terrible war, with its countless soldiers can begin, there will be an invasion from outer space! Jesus is coming again! The heavens will rend asunder, and the multiplied millions at Megeddo will catch a momentary glimpse of Glory. One word from the returning Christ is all it will take and the war will be won. The Lord will take personal charge of this poor, old, lost world of ours and the oft-recited prayer will be answered at last: "Thy Kingdom come, Thy will be done, on earth as it is in Heaven!" The hour is drawing nigh.

THE LORD IS MY SHEPHERD
PSALM 23

This is everybody's psalm. First, we are in the glen, then, in the gorge and, finally, we are in the Glory. The Psalm tells us about the fold, and about the foe, and about the future. It gives us the three-fold secret of happiness. It begins with THE SECRET OF A HAPPY LIFE. Our Shepherd takes care of all of our needs. He takes care of all our <u>secular</u> needs. He leads us beside the still waters and into the green pastures. And He takes care of all our <u>spiritual</u> needs. He "restores our soul" and gives us needed righteousness. "He brings back my soul" is the way one translation renders it. And, at what cost! As the old hymn puts it:

> *"None of the ransomed ever knew*
> *How deep were the waters crossed,*
> *Nor how dark was the night that*
> *the Lord passed through*
> *E're He found His sheep that was lost."*

The psalm continues with THE SECRET OF A HAPPY DEATH. We come now, in the psalm, to the valley of the shadow of death. We notice at once that there is a dramatic change in the pronouns. Up to now the psalmist has been saying: "He! He! He!" He has been talking <u>about</u> the Shepherd. Now He says, "Thou! Thou! Thou!" As the dark valley looms, the Shepherd comes closer. Now the psalmist is no longer talking about Him, he is talking <u>to</u> Him.

And, behold, the threatening valley turns out to be no more than the valley of the <u>shadow</u> of death. The shadow of a dog cannot bite. The shadow of a sword cannot kill. The shadow of death cannot harm the child of God.

Where there is a shadow, however, there has to be a substance. We discover that the substance of death is very close by, right there in the previous psalm—"My God, My God, why hast Thou forsaken Me?" That, indeed, is the substance of death, to be forsaken by God forever.

But there is something else, too, where there is a shadow, there also has to be a light. It is the light shining on the substance that casts the shadow.

Some years ago I heard a letter read in church. It had just been received from a beloved medical missionary who was dying of leukemia. He wrote: "David, in Psalm 23, talks about the valley of the shadow of death. Fellow saints of God, I have come into the valley. But there is no shadow. On the contrary, I have found that 'the path of the just is as a shining light which shineth more and more unto the perfect day'" (Prov.4:18). That is the secret of a happy death.

Finally, we have here THE SECRET OF A HAPPY ETERNITY. "I shall dwell in the house of the Lord forever." That is David's final offering.

Harriet Beecher Stowe, who wrote Uncle Tom's Cabin, did more to strike the shackles off America's slaves than any other book or cause. In one of many dramatic scenes she shows us poor Uncle Tom in the merciless hands of the cruel Simon Legree. The malicious slave owner was determined to break the will of the kindly Uncle Tom. When he refused to be cruel to the other slaves, even when commanded to thrash them by Legree's direct command, Legree threatened him with torture. "How would you like to have a slow fire built around you, Tom?" he said. "I know you can do many cruel things, Master," said Uncle Tom. "You can even kill me. But there's all eternity to come after that. That was the heavenly vision which filled the soul of Uncle Tom with bliss and the soul of Simon Legree with terror.

F. W. Boreham reminds us of what old Rabbi Duncan used to say to his students at the turn of the year: "Gentlemen," he would say, "your friends will be wishing you a happy New Year. Your old Rabbi wishes you a happy eternity." Jesus does better than that. He assures us a happy eternity.

ENTER INTO REST

HEBREWS 4:11

Years ago a missionary friend of mine was bumping along a backwoods African trail in a pickup truck. He saw a native up ahead, carrying a big bundle on his head. He stopped and asked him if he's like a ride. The native scrambled into the back of the pickup, and off they went. Presently, the missionary glanced in his rearview mirror and saw the man standing up, still holding the heavy load on his head. He stopped. "Why don't you put your load down?" he asked. "Oh," said the man, "I didn't know your truck could carry both me and my load!"

That reminds us of many Christians. They do not think that salvation includes putting down their load, whatever that load might be and however heavy it might be. They have not learned the lesson of Hebrews 4, that God loves to give rest to His own.

First there is CREATION REST. "God did rest," we read, "on the seventh day." With a rush and a roar, the universe sprang into being. Astronomers set before us the picture of countless stars and their satellites traveling at inconceivable velocities, on prodigious orbits, expending near inexhaustible reservoirs of energy. But it was God who flung these vast galactic empires into space. He summoned the light to shine and made the darkness to flee. He separated the waters. He raised the continents. He brought forth life in a myriad forms. He crowned all this activity with the creation of man.

Then He rested. Not because He was tired. He never gets tired. It took just ten words in Genesis 1:1 to record the original creative act. The brevity of the narrative matches the economy with which omnipotence expends its power. So God rested, not because He was tired, but because the work was done!

Then there is CANAAN REST. "They shall not enter into my rest!" That was God's verdict upon Israel at Kadesh Barnea. He had brought them out. He had brought them through. Now He wanted to bring them in. There before them was the Promised Land. But by this time, the Hebrews had heard of the giants; and they dug in their heels. "Take us back to Egypt," they said. We'd be better off in the wilderness." So God let them have their way; and for forty long years, until all that doubting generation was dead, they roamed the wilderness. They had trusted God to bring them out, but they doubted that God could bring them in. How sad! That generation never experienced Canaan rest.

Then, there is COVENANT REST: "For He spake in a certain place of the seventh day on this wise: And God did rest the seventh day from all His works."

The Sabbath was an essential part of the Mosaic Covenant. At Sinai God determined to share His own Sabbath rest with His blood-bought people. On the seventh day of each week the people could turn aside from the daily concerns of the work-a-day world to enjoy fellowship with God. God deemed this weekly Sabbath rest so important, indeed, that He appended the death sentence to it for those who desecrated it. We know all too well what happened. The rabbis so meddled with the Sabbath that it became a burden rather than a blessing, and God ended up abolishing the whole thing.

Now we have CALVARY REST: "There remaineth therefore a rest to the people of God." Our rest is not in a day, but in a deliverance; not in a weekly Sabbath, but in God's wonderful Son. When He had finished the work God gave Him to do, He cried, "It is finished!" And so it is. Done is the work that saves.

As one of his great gospel crusades came to an end, D. L. Moody was accosted by a belated seeker. Already work crews were carting off the chairs and demolishing the platform. "Mr. Moody," said the late enquirer, "what must I do to be saved?" "You're too late," the evangelist replied. "Surely I'm not too late," the man said. "Oh yes," said Mr. Moody, "you're too late. You're two thousand years too late. If you want to do something, you're too late. It's all been done!" And he pointed the man to Christ and to Calvary rest. As the hymn says:

> "Lord Jesus Thou hast promised rest,
> Then give it now to Thee,
> The rest of ceasing from myself
> To find my all in Thee."

THE UNSEEN WORLD
LUKE 16

There is a vocabulary of half a dozen words in the Greek text of the Bible to depict for us various facts about the underworld. First, there is the word Hades and its equivalent Hebrew word Sheol. The basic idea behind the word <u>Sheol</u> is "the grave" (as distinguished from "a grave," a mere burying place). The word occurs sixty-five times in the Old Testament. The word Hades, which occurs eleven times in the New Testament, means "the unseen." Both Sheol and Hades refer to the abode of the dead, and both give the impression of it being in a downward direction. Samuel, for instance, castigated King Saul for bringing him "up" when he sought spiritist did from the witch of Endo (1 Sam. 28:15). At death, the Lord Jesus "descended" into the lower parts of the earth (Eph.4:8-11).

The incident of the rich man and Lazarus (Luke 16) tells us much about Hades. In Jesus' day, it was in two sections divided by a great gulf. The rich man was on one side in a place of torment. Lazarus was on the other side. He had been carried by the angels to "Abraham's bosom," a Hebrew idiom for a place of rest, fellowship and happiness. The rich man was consciously lost. He was in agony and he was anxious for his lost brothers. He learned he was beyond help or hope. Abraham's side of the gulf, was known as "paradise," a word which suggests a park-like abode of bliss.

At the time of Christ's ascension, the paradise section of Hades seems to have been moved to a different place. Paul was "caught up" to it (2 Cor.12:4) and experienced things which were beyond description. In one way they were of a material nature because Paul thought himself to be still "in the body." In another way they were of a mystical nature because he thought himself to be "out of the body." From then on, Paul had a strong desire to return to that place and to be with Christ which, he said, was "far better." The expression can be rendered "far, far better." The use of the superlative emphasizes the joy that awaits us there (Phil.2:23).

Another word is <u>Gehenna</u> (<u>Tophet</u> in the Old Testament). This word refers to the final abode of the wicked dead. It is called "the lake of fire" at the end of the Apocalypse (Rev.20:14). The Greek word is a transliteration of the Hebrew word <u>Gai Hinnom</u>, "the valley of Hinnom, where apostate Jews sacrificed their children to idols on the red-hot lap of Moloch (1 Kings 11:7). King Josiah put an end to the practice. The site itself was a place where three valleys united south of Jerusalem. In Jesus' day, it was the city garbage dump; and fires burned there continually consuming the dross. It became a synonym and type of Hell and its unquenchable fire (Mark 9:43-48).

At the great white throne judgment, death and Hades will be emptied into the lake of fire as the bodies and souls of the wicked dead will be reunited and cast into Hell itself (Rev.20:14).

The Hebrew word for "Heaven" comes from a root word which is the usual word for the sky. The corresponding Greek word became the name for God's home. The idea of heaven occurs often in the New Testament. We are to pray, for instance, to "our Father which art in heaven." John, in the Apocalypse, saw "a door opened in heaven." Heaven is a real place. Jesus said it contains many mansions (John 14:2). The description given of the celestial city (Rev.4-5; 21-22) gives us our best impression of what heaven will be like. We shall dwell in heaven in our resurrection bodies in "joy unspeakable and full of glory" (1 Peter 1:8).

The word Tartarus is used only by Peter, and it refers to the prison house of the worst of the fallen angels (2 Peter 2:4). These not only supported Satan in his initial rebellion, they lusted after human women and helped debauch the world of Noah's day (Gen.6:4; Jud 6-7).

There is one other word, Abussos (the Abyss). It is the place where evil spirits of great malevolence and power are incarcerated for now (Rev.9:1-12) and where Satan will be imprisoned during the Millennium (Rev.20:1-3).

The unseen world is real. We need to make sure we belong to the Lord Jesus Who has the keys of death and Hades and Who, alone, is the way to Heaven. "No man cometh unto the Father but by Me," He says (John 14:6).

TEN SHEKELS AND A SUIT
JUDGES 17-18

Judas sold Jesus for thirty pieces of silver. Jonathan, the grandson of Moses, sold his soul for ten shekels and a suit. The introduction of apostasy into Israel was AN INFAMOUS THING. It all began in a small way. A man named Micah stole 1100 shekels of silver from his mother. Frightened by her curses, he confessed and restored the money. His mother took two hundred shekels and had them made into idols. Micah put them in a shrine.

About this time, a wandering Levite from Bethlehem showed up. Micah saw an opportunity to legitimize his false religion. He propositioned the Levite. "Come and dwell with me," he said. "I will promote you from being a mere Levite be being my priest. I will feed you, and I will give you ten shekels of silver and a suit." The Levite's name was Jonathan. His father was Gershom, the son of Moses (1 Chr.23:15). He was a contemporary of Phinehas, the grandson of Aaron, who is mentioned in his capacity of high priest as making inquiry before the Lord at a time of national crisis.

Thus early did apostasy rear its head in Israel. It seems incredible that Moses' own grandson should be at the heart of this infamous thing. Once Micah had installed Jonathan as priest of his new religion, he felt he had legitimized it: "Now I know that the Lord will do me good, seeing I have a Levite to be my priest," he said. He and his hired Levite had forgotten the second commandment: "Thou shalt not make unto thee any graven image, or any likeness of anything that is in heaven above, or that is in the earth beneath, or that is in the water under the earth. Thou shalt not bow down thyself to them, nor serve them: for I the Lord thy God am a jealous God, visiting the iniquity of the fathers upon the children unto the third and fourth generation of them that hate me; And showing mercy unto thousands of them that love me, and keep my commandments" (Ex.20:4-6).

Thus idolatry took root. It was an infamous thing, it was also AN INFECTIOUS THING for, from being a family affair, it soon became a tribal affair. The tribe of Dan still had not settled in the territory assigned to it by God. It so happened that a band of landless Danites came across Jonathan, the Judean Levite. It seems that they knew him. They were certainly curious about his new occupation and intrigued by his reply. The six hundred armed Danites were swift to make up their minds. "Forget this fellow, Micah," they said. "Come with us. We'll make you priest to a whole tribe. Go and get the fellow's gods." The apostate Levite, a grandson of Moses, called of God to defend the Mosaic Law, was delighted. "The priest's heart was glad," the Holy Spirit says. His fortune was made! And his was judgment sure.

Thus idolatry proved itself an infectious thing. The Danites "set them up Micah's graven image which he had made, all the time that the house of God was in Shiloh."

Ten shekels and a suit! Thus cheaply an apostate Levite sold his soul, and seemingly prospered. Soon the infection of apostasy spread to the whole nation of Israel. The days of the Judges saw the virus incubate and spread. It was cleared up by David but broke out again under Solomon and in the end it doomed the monarchy. It all began with ten shekels and a shirt.

Now then, Jonathan, go and explain yourself to Moses and to God on the judgment side of death.

A VERY REAL PROBLEM

ROMANS 7

There are three men in Romans 7. There is the spiritual man (7:1-6), the one who, "married to another," brings forth "fruit unto God." There is the natural man, Paul as he was in his unregenerate days (7:7-13—all the verbs here are in the past tense). Finally, there is the carnal man (7:14-25), the "wretched man" who knows the theology of the victorious life but who is unable to make it work in practice. Paul brings his keen mind to bear on this problem, a mind in tune with the Holy Spirit.

First, he goes back to his unregenerate days. He reviews his career as A DOOMED SINNER. He was condemned by the Law. In those days, he had tried to produce a standard of behavior God could accept, by his own efforts at keeping God's law, only to discover that the Law did four things that were against him.

The Law revealed sin. Paul said, "I had not known sin but by the Law—I had not known lust except the Law had said, Thou shalt not covet." He could run his eye down the list of the Ten Commandments and claim to have kept the first nine. The tenth commandment said, "Thou shalt have no evil desire," and that one slew him. And he knew it.

The Law revived sin. "When the commandment came sin revived, and I died", Paul said. How true that is! We see a sign which reads: "Keep off the grass" or "Don't touch." Before we see the sign, we have no thought of doing either one or the other. But when we see the forbidding sign, that is the very thing we want to do!

The Law <u>rewards</u> sin. It does not reward us for keeping its commandments because we are supposed to do that. The Law of God expects us to do what it says. It rewards us with punishment when we break its decrees. It is a stern taskmaster. It does not bend the rules.

Finally, the Law <u>rebukes</u> sin. The Law is "holy, just and good," Paul says. Moreover, it makes sin exceeding sinful" because, in the last analysis, all sin is high treason against God.

So, there he was, a natural man, a DOOMED SINNER, <u>condemned by the Law</u> and unable to meet even heaven's MINIMUM demands.

Now Paul reviews his career as a DEFEATED SAINT, <u>conquered by lust</u>. Again his dissects his behavior. He comes up with four spiritual laws.

First, there is <u>the law of Sinai</u>. That law, the law of God, pointed him heavenward and made it clear to him that God demands perfection, not only in keeping the letter of the law, but also in keeping the spirit of the law as expounded in the Sermon on the Mount.

There is, also <u>the law of sin</u>—"I find then a law" says Paul, "that when I would do good, evil is present with me." The "law of sin pulled him downwards. These two laws tore him apart. But there was more.

There is what Paul calls "<u>the law of my mind</u>": With his mind he consented unto the law that it was good. His mind paid tribute to God's law. He agreed that he should live the way God told him to live. He endorsed God's law with his mind. He should live a holy life. He should exhibit a perfect standard of behavior.

But there is also what Paul calls "<u>the law of my members</u>." His bodily members took sides with the law of sin. His eyes looked with lust, his ears delighted in gossip. So much so he was virtually torn apart by these conflicting laws. More, he discovered that, as a defeated saint, he was doing exactly the same thing he had done as a doomed sinner. He was still trying in his own strength to produce the kind of life God expects.

Then he discovered the secret. "It is through Jesus Christ our Lord," he cried! It is trusting, not trying. The same Christ Who gave him <u>eternal</u> life now offered him <u>victorious life</u>. "I thank God," was Paul's final sigh of blessed relief.

SONS OF GOD
ROMANS 8:14-39

When the widow Douglas adopted Huckleberry Finn, it turned out to be a painful process for the boy. His father had been the town drunk and the boy himself a picturesque prodigal. His home was an old hogshead. His food such scraps as he could scrounge. His spicy language was the delight of all the other boys and the horror of their parents. His pipe, his tattered ruin of rags which constituted his wardrobe, his unkempt person did not qualify him for society.

The widow set about adopting him, and then adapting him. He had to be washed and dressed in clothes which tortured him, and shod with shoes which cramped him. He had to sleep in a bed at night, sit up at table for his meals and use a knife and fork. The whole process hurt.

When God adopts us into His family it is the same. We have to be adapted to our new life in Christ. So the Holy Spirit sets to work on us. We have to be groomed for glory.

Let us meditate on what it means to be placed into God's family as adult sons by the process of adoption. Three things happen. First, we are led by the Spirit (14). We, who have been adopted into God's family have this common trait that are guided through life by the Spirit of God. Even though we may stumble and fall, nevertheless, obedience to the Spirit is the main trend of our life. Take the Mississippi River, for instance. Even though it flows southward there are places where it flows eastward and even northward. But these are only temporary aberrations. The main southward direction of the flows always takes over in the end. It is just so with a child of God. The true flow of a believer's life is towards holiness, even though there may be occasional lapses. In time the flow heavenward and homeward is resumed.

Then, too, we are loved by the Father (15-16). The Holy spirit bears witness to that with our human spirit. Paul says, we are to address God as "Abba Father." "Abba" is an Aramaic word, which expresses the cry of an infant. It is the word of unquestioning trust. The word "Father" comes from the Greek (pater). It is the form of address used by an adult son who is able to enter into the heart, mind and will of the Father. Jesus used both words in Gethsemane. It is proof of our sonship that we can do the same.

Finally, we are lifted by the Son (17). "If children, then heirs of God, and joint heirs with Christ . . ." Paul adds, "if so be that we suffer with Him that we may also be glorified together" (v. 17). There is always a strong link in the Bible between the sufferings of Christ, and the glory that is to follow. We see this principle illustrated in the lives of Peter and Paul. Peter was a witness of the sufferings and a partaker of the glory (on the Mount of Transfiguration). Paul was a witness of the glory (on the Damascus road) and a partaker of the sufferings. God allows us to suffer in order to purify us and lift us.

When God met Jacob at the Jabbok He broke him in order to bless him (Gen. 32:24-32). Carnal, scheming, self-willed Jacob was renamed "Israel." He was proclaimed to be "a prince with God and with men". This crisis experience, however, was followed by a long, slow process of adapting Jacob. It took time. It always does. There are no shortcuts to a holy life.

In chapter after chapter of Genesis we see the process. There was the defilement of his daughter (something which must have broken Jacob's heart). There was the duplicity of Simeon and Levi. There was the disgrace of Reuben, the degradation of Reuben, the disappearance of Joseph, the detention of Reuben in Egypt and the demand for Benjamin. The process went on and on. Nor do we see much change in Jacob, not until we get near the end.

In the closing chapters of Genesis, however, we see a different Jacob. We see a man adapted for glory. He too, was in Egypt now. He was surrounded by wealth and opportunity. He was there for seventeen years and could have made his fortune. But his heart was in another land. His heart was in Canaan, untouched by all the gold and glamour of Egypt. More than that, we see him blessing Pharaoh on his throne and bearing witness to his pilgrimage. He was ready for heaven and home. So we learn that God adapts those he adopts, and that He is never in a hurry, He takes his time.

THE LITTLE FLOCK

LUKE 12:32

"Fear not little flock, for it is the Father's good pleasure to give us the Kingdom."

The background of this statement is the parable of the rich fool whose rosy prospects were all built upon a fatal delusion. All this prosperous farmer could think about was his bursting barns. He had "much goods," it says. He thought also that he had "many years." The poor fool. Little did he know it but he was to be dead before another sunrise.

By contrast with this rich fool there are the Lord's disciples, poor and weak and in a hostile world; but rich towards God. The Lord paints three pictures for them in less than a dozen and a half words.

There is a picture of a little flock, of no account in the world's scale of values, but of vast importance in God's. A little flock! Not a herd, not a swarm, not a pack, but a flock. And a little flock at that. God's people never become an overwhelming majority in this world. David's brothers sneered: "With whom have you left those few sheep in the wilderness?" Napoleon once said, "God is on the side of the big battalions." More fool Napoleon.

The world forgets the basic fact that the little flock it so despises is God's little flock. The Lord Jesus appears in the Apocalypse as a little lamb (Rev.5:6), in appearance as a slain lamb. But let no one forget that this little lamb has seven horns (omnipotence) and seven eyes (omniscience) and that Satan's great red dragon is no match for Him. God stopped Napoleon with a snowflake, and snowflake after snowflake, until his conquering armies ground to a halt, surrounded by snowflakes and frozen with the cold.

Then there is a picture of A LOVING FATHER. "Fear not little flock, it is your Father's good pleasure to give you the kingdom." God is referred to as a Father only about four or five times in the entire Old Testament. He was known by many mighty and magnificent names, but none of them compared with this new name Jesus brought with Him to earth—"Father!" God is "our Father," He said. In the Lord's incomparable twin parable of the prodigal and his elder brother the name "father" occurs twelve times

(Lk.15:11-32). So the picture of a flock is replaced now by the picture of a family. The God and Father of our Lord Jesus Christ is now our God and Father. Moreover it is His good pleasure to provide and protect and plan, and all for our present and eternal bliss.

Finally, there is a picture of A LOFTY FUTURE. "It is your Father's good pleasure to give you the kingdom." It is a long way from the pasture to the palace. David made it. So shall we.

It has always been God's purpose to establish a kingdom in this world. When He created Adam He gave him "dominion" (Gen.1:26). Throughout the Old Testament period He pursued that purpose. Israel's first attempt to establish a monarch was disastrous. They chose a king after their own, rebellious hearts. Then David came, "a man after God's own heart." Had it not been for the disastrous Bathsheba affair, David might well have conquered all the Promised Land, from the Nile to the Euphrates. The long apostasy riddled history of the earthly kingdom climaxed in the fall of both Israel and Judah. The monarchy became the Dependency and the land fell under foreign rule.

Then Jesus came. John the Baptist proclaimed Him as the long-awaited Messiah. Had the Jewish people accepted Him, the Empire of Christ would have spread throughout the world. They rejected Him. "We have no king but Caesar" they said to Pontius Pilate. Pilate knew better. He wrote his own title for the cross: "This is Jesus of Nazareth, The King of the Jews."

During this present age, God's Kingdom purposes are in abeyance. He is building a church and His kingdom is essentially spiritual (Jno.3:3, 5-8) in nature.

But the King is coming back. The Kingdom will come. Jesus will reign. And when He does enter into His Kingdom so shall we. It is the Father's good pleasure to guarantee that.

GO FORWARD

Moses was all too familiar with the atmosphere of Pharaoh's court. He had been raised in it and, moreover, was "learned in all the wisdom of the Egyptians" (Acts 7:22). The scholars who took Moses in hand, at the request of Pharaoh's daughter, had their work cut out for them for what they taught was contrary to what his own mother had taught. When he came to manhood, he rejected the wisdom, the wealth and the ways of Egypt. He was not impressed by a later Pharaoh's scornful, "I know not the Lord." Pharaoh thought he was a God, Ra, the incarnation of the sun. But if this Pharaoh did not know the Lord, Moses did. And that was the difference between them. Moses knew God, therefore, Pharaoh was no match for him. By the time Moses was finished with him, having visited him with plague after plague and having left him at last with a dead child in every Egyptian home, Pharaoh was terrified both of Moses, and his God. At least he was terrified for twenty-four hours or so.

The Pharaoh of Moses' day was the great, red dragon of the Nile. He was controlled by "the spirit that now worketh in the children of disobedience" and Pharaoh had his army and thousands of men to march at his word. Moses had a little lamb, a Passover lamb. The various miracles of Moses did not bring about Israel's release. They only made the monarch made. He was broken at last by means of the death of the lamb. Its blood was shed, its body was impaled upon a cross. It was roasted with fire and founded a feast for the people of God.

The people believed God and some three million of them were saved in one spectacular night. Israel was "a nation born in a day." The emancipated people marched out of Egypt by the thousand, carrying with them a sizable share of the wealth of the land. The sight and sound of them disappearing behind the same dunes was too much for the Egyptian king. He reacted against his decision to let them go. He mobilized his men! He marched after them! He would bring them back! He would make them pay! The born fools were heading for the sea! He would trap them there with his soldiers behind and the Red Sea before.

All too soon Pharaoh had forgotten about God. The intended military move, of encirclement followed by a swift cavalry charge, was halted by a miracle. As though Pharaoh had not had more than enough of miracles. The Shekinah glory cloud, which had been leading Israel, now moved to the rear and stood between the Egyptians and their prey. The fiery cloudy pillar was the visible token that God was on Israel's side. To get at the people the Egyptian cavalry would first need to get past God Himself. And

Pharaoh, puppet god of Egypt as he imagined himself to be, was no match for the true and living God.

"Go forward!" That was God's words to His people. But how? That was the problem. Then it happened. A wide way opened up through the sea, and seizing their opportunity they crossed over. The foolhardy Egyptians seized what looked like a golden opportunity to overwhelm the fleeing Hebrews. The Shekinah pillar stood aside making way for the Egyptians to march. The crack cavalry troops of the Egyptian army lashed their horses. The chariots and horsemen surged into the gap between the piled up seas. Then disaster struck them. The wheels fell off their chariots rendering them useless and waters suddenly returned. The Egyptians perished in the sea.

The pathway to Canaan now opened before the victorious Israelites. They followed the guiding pillar. It led them along a grand hiway—separation, security, sanctification!

First there was separation. The water of the Red Sea came between the Hebrews and their old way of life. Next there was song.—"Thus the Lord saved Israel" we read. "Then sang Moses and the children of Israel." Security followed as a matter of course—their every need was met by miracle after miracle: bread from heaven! water from the riven rock! victory over Amalek! Then, finally, there was sanctification. The redeemed Israelites were brought to Sinai and taught how to order their lives. Moreover God Himself came down and pitched His tent in the midst of His own, to walk with them, and talk with them, and treat them like no other nation on earth. All these blessings were heaped up for them along the wilderness way. All this and Canaan, too!

When God says, "Go forward," it is always best to obey.

AN INNUMERABLE COMPANY

HEBREWS 12:22-23

"You are come," says the apostle, "to an innumerable company of angels, to the general assembly and church of the firstborn . . ." Here we have two vast populations and two different orders. There are those in heaven by right of <u>creation</u>, the heavenly native born hosts; and there are those in heaven by right of <u>redemption</u>, the blood-bought human hosts.

Think first of the HEAVENLY HOSTS. John tells us that there are ten thousand times ten thousand of them and thousands of thousands (Rev.5:11). In other words, they are countless, a multitude that no man can number. Heaven is their home and holiness is the breath of their being. They are mentioned over one hundred times in the Old Testament and 165 times in the New.

There are <u>messenger</u> angels, Gabriel, for instance. There are <u>minister-ing</u> angels, "ministering spirits" is the way the Holy Spirit describes them. As such they visited Abraham in his tent, delivered Lot from Sodom, escorted Jacob back to the Promised Land and protected him from Laban's spite. Then, too, there are <u>martial</u> angels, headed by Michael, the Archangel, active in the wars of the Lord and in end-time events.

The rightful home of these exalted beings is in heaven, a land of fade-less day, where they pave their streets with gold and built their walls of jasper, where they count not time by years, and where Christ sits on the right hand of the majesty on high. What stories they will have to tell us when we arrive in heaven when they recount the ways in which, all unknown to us, they ministered to our needs on our journey home.

But the Holy Spirit mentions another company in heaven, the HUMAN HOSTS, made up of men and women, boys and girls, washed in the blood of the Lamb and made it fit for the holiness and happiness of heaven. He sees two such companies.

There is "the general assembly of the firstborn." The word used is paneguris. It was used in classical Greek of a festive gathering. It appears to be employed here to describe a convocation, convened in heaven, to do honor to the saints of God, particularly to that special company of the redeemed who comprise the Bride of Christ.

In the Old Testament the firstborn of both men and beast was to be set apart for God (Ex.13:13, 15; 34:20). If of man, the child was to be redeemed. If of a clean beast, it was to be sacrificed. If unclean, it either had its neck broken or it was redeemed by a lamb. Later the tribe of Levi was chosen from among the tribes of Israel and its members substituted for the general firstborn (Num.3:12, 41, 46;8:13-19).

Special privileges accrued to the firstborn. To the firstborn son belonged the birthright which included headship of the family, the right to be the family priest and, in the early days, the right to be the progenitor of Christ. It also included a double portion of the Father's property.

Viewed in relation to the Gentile nations, God called Israel "My son, even My firstborn" (Ex.4:22). Pharaoh was warned that if he refused to acknowledge this primacy among the nations of the Hebrew people, then God would slay his son, even his firstborn. And, even more mysterious and terrible that that, God would single out all the firstborn Egyptian males and all the first born beasts in the barn and in the fields, and slay them too (Ex.11:5).

"The general assembly of the firstborn" mentioned here are the Jewish friends of the bridegroom. Paul foresaw the day when, in the ages to come, God would show the exceeding riches of His grace in His kindness toward us through Christ Jesus (Eph.2:7). The angels will marvel at this proof of God's grace. Saints of other ages will marvel, too.

Closely linked with "this general assembly of God's Old Testament firstborn ones" is "the church of the firstborn which are written in heaven." Here we have the raptured and ascended church, the Bride of Christ, taking the highest place that heaven affords, and being seated with Christ far above all principalities and powers and every name that is named. "Rejoice," said Jesus to His disciples, "that your name is written in heaven!" Think of it! Our names written there! That acknowledges us as children of God, as joint-heirs with Christ and as members of the aristocracy of Heaven! "There!" David would have said, had such a truth been revealed to Him. "There, send that to the Chief Musician!" That is something to sing about down here, even as they sing about it over there.

YE ARE COME TO MOUNT ZION
HEBREWS 12:22

Mount Zion! That is WHAT it is. The apostle puts it in stark contrast with Mount Sinai. Sinai was a place to turn blood to ice. The earth rolled and tumbled beneath Moses' feet at Sinai until even he quaked with terror before the Lord. From nowhere, yet from everywhere, had come the disembodied voice, with its dictates and demands, its warnings and its woes, its rituals, rules and regulations. Sinai was no place to visit, much less to live.

Thankfully, we are transported in a moment to Mount Zion. The name is familiar to us from our Old Testament history books, where it is mentioned some one hundred and fifty times. It is a place often identified with the earthly city of Jerusalem. The earthly zion, however, is but a picture of the heavenly one.

During the millennial reign, this celestial city, the heavenly Jerusalem, will come down and take up its place in the sky, in a space-time dimension, immediately above the earthly Jerusalem. That is <u>what</u> it is. Mount Zion is a real place for real people. It is the home of the blood-bought saints of God. We call it heaven.

Think, too, of WHOSE it is. It is "the city of the living God." The earthly Jerusalem was known as "the City of David" (1 Kings 3:1). The heavenly Jerusalem is known as "the City of God."

This is the city which captured the imagination of Abraham (Heb.11:10). We know from the book of Genesis about the <u>voice</u> that spoke to Abraham, the voice that demanded he turn his back on Ur of the Chaldees, step out by faith, and become a pilgrim and a stranger on the earth. That voice turned his feet towards the Promised Land of Canaan. It is not until we are well into the New Testament that we learn about the <u>vision</u>. The vision turned his heart towards heaven at the same time that it turned his heart towards Canaan. "He went out," says the Holy Spirit, "for he looked for a city which hath foundations, whose builder and maker is God." Ever afterwards Abraham had a new focus. This world was not his home, he was just a-passing through. His treasures were laid up, somewhere beyond the blue.

Abraham was seventy-five when God called him <u>out</u>, from Ur of the Chaldees. One hundred years later, God called him <u>home</u>—to the city of the living God. It is an <u>impregnable</u> city with towering jasper walls. It is an <u>immense</u> city, fifteen hundred miles in all directions. It is an imperial city where stands the great white throne. It is an <u>imperishable</u> city, engineered for eternity.

Finally, let us think WHERE it is. It is called "the <u>heavenly</u> Jerusalem." The word used is epouranios, literally "above the sky." The word conveys the thought of something very high. Psalm 75:6, Isaiah 14:13 and Job 26:7 all point toward the far and distant north. We project our line beyond the northward-pointing axis of the earth on into space; beyond the North Pole, beyond the polar star (which orientates the geography of earth and sky) and lo, out there, lies that city four square.

> *"A tent or a cottage—why should I care?*
> *They're building a palace for me over there*
> *Tho' exiled from home, yet still I may sing*
> *All glory to God, I'm a child of the King."*

THE POSTMAN FROM PATMOS AT EPHESUS

REVELATION 2:1-7

It had been a great church, Paul's climax church, indeed, his best church, born in a Holy Ghost revival. The whole area, for many miles around, had felt that awakening. Churches had sprung up like mushrooms on the moor. Paul's letter to Ephesus contains the most glorious truths ever revealed to men. Paul, Timothy and John had all ministered there. It had an eldership of godly men, trained and taught by Paul, forewarned and challenged by him and charged by him to watch out for the wolves.

By the time John wrote, the wolves were already playing havoc with the flock in other parts of the world. Thanks to its wise and watchful elders, they had not yet done much damage at Ephesus. But they were lurking around, snarling in the shadows, eager to move in. Anyone wanting to get into that church, however, must first get past the elders, no easy task.

We can picture the same postman from Patmos as he arrives at this, the first of seven sister churches on his list. At the door of the church, he is met by one of the elders. Perhaps he was one of those men who, forty years before, had met the master at Miletos. The conversation would go something like this:

"Good morning!"

"Good morning!"

"I am Barnabas of Ephesus. Who are you?"

"Me? I'm Lucius of Rome, a courier and a Christian."

"So, you're a Christian. How were you saved?"

He gives his testimony.

"Have you been baptized?"

"Oh, yes!"

"What think ye of Christ?" "Where do you stand on the inerrancy of Scripture?" And so on and on. He was given a thorough grilling before being allowed to take his place in the church. The elders were watching for the wolves. They were STANDING UP FOR THE TRUTH.

The postman found himself a seat. As he looked around, he saw some of the Nicolaitans, a group of semi-professional functionaries who wore distinctive clothing and who seemed to have a monopoly of sort on preaching and praying, a kind of embryonic clergy. The church as a whole, however, seemed to be STANDING UP TO THE TEST. For, so far, this tendency to divide between clergy and laity was in its infancy and not too sure of itself.

But what impressed the postman most was the long list of announcements of coming church activities and events. They seemed to be endless. There was something going on all the time. The church was STANDING UP TO THE TASK. It was indeed a very busy church.

But now the service was over, and one of the robed officials read the benediction. The postman from Patmos jumped to his feet. "Excuse me, my brothers," we can hear him say, "I have just been over to Patmos. I've seen the apostle John. He has a letter for you. I'll read it. It's very brief."

The central message of the letter was to the point: "I know all about you," Jesus said. "You are a fundamental, Bible-believing church, and you are a very busy church. But I have something against you. You people do not love _Me_ anymore. And that is so serious that, unless there is a Holy Ghost revival at Ephesus, I'm going to close you down. I have no use for a church that doesn't love _Me_ any more."

How many of our busy, fundamentalist churches, we wonder, could stand that test, the vital test of love? Poor, insolvent Ephesus! All the coin of her spiritual commerce was revealed as worthless, counterfeit and spurious. It never came from the royal mint of love.

THE POSTMAN FROM PATMOS AT SMYRNA

REVELATION 2:8-11

The postman from Patmos might have found it difficult to discover where the church at Smyrna met. Christians were not popular in those parts, so their meeting place was not likely to be advertised. The believers witnessed, of course; but they found it prudent to keep a low profile. When the postman did succeed in finding their meeting place he would most certainly have been required to give full proof of his integrity. He may even have had to show them John's letter and signature.

He soon sorted out the saints, however, once his credentials had been endorsed and he was shown to his seat. Over there, for instance, were some broken men. Indeed, there were quite a number of them, men who had evidently known the pain of persecution for they bore in their bodies the marks of suffering. And there were empty seats, too, and widows and orphans, all the usual proofs of persecution—people broken in body, if not in spirit.

Then, too, there were some bankrupt men, evidently poor in this world's goods. They, too, seemed to be a numerous group, people who had suffered the loss of all things and who now lived off the charity of the church. There were Jewish believers among them, excommunicated by the synagogue and plundered of all they possessed. And there were Gentile believers whose goods and homes had been confiscated by the state, outlawed for refusing to put a pinch of salt on Caesar's altar in the market place.

But, over yonder, was yet another group of people, blasphemous men no less. Of all the strange things, these people around him, had espoused a strange form of heresy. They were Gentiles who had embraced Judaism and who nevertheless considered themselves to be Christians. As if it were not enough for the church to be persecuted by outsiders, now it had apostasy within. The Lord described their particular circle of "fellowship" as "the synagogue of Satan." They had turned away from the truth. They were not Jews returning to the synagogue, though that would have been bad enough. These were Gentiles who had crucified to themselves the Son of

God afresh and put him to an open shame (Heb.6:4-6). They had embraced a Christ-rejecting religion, submitted to circumcision, embraced the Law as a system, elevated the Sabbath and proclaimed themselves to be Jews. But they were not Jews. Nor were they Christians. They belonged to the synagogue of Satan, a synagogue created by Satan to snare them.

Thankfully, the postman from Patmos saw yet another group of men, bold men, men undaunted by the persecution which was already their lot in life. "Tribulation ten days." Thus the Holy spirit sums up the brief but fierce time of persecution which awaited His church. Stripes and imprisonment awaited them, but they would be faithful unto death. And for all such, the promise of the Lord was that they would receive a crown of life.

The postman must have marveled at such a collection of people. The Lord appropriately addressed this congregation as the one "which was dead and is alive." And He promised that its overcomes would not be hurt of the second death.

Most churches today have the same odd mixture of truth and error, of faith and fear, of conviction and compromise. We must be overcomers, victorious believers triumphing over foes within and without, faithful in the face of persecution, determined one day to wear a crown.

THE POSTMAN FROM PATMOS AT PERGAMOS
REVELATION 2:12-17

At Smyrna the postman from Patmos had discovered Satan's At Smyrna the postman from Patmos had discovered Satan's synagogue, right there in the church. At Pergamos he discovered Satan's seat. For many years now the cult of the ancient pagan mysteries, long centered at Babylon, had been housed at Pergamos. It was an important power-base of the Evil One. From Pergamos he energized and directed the idolatrous worship of all the world's pagan religions.

The church had invaded the world, born of wind and flame, injected suddenly and sublimely into history in Jerusalem. Satan's goal, of course, was to retaliate. The advent of the church had taken him completely by surprise at Pentecost. It's victorious banners were springing up everywhere in the world—and the world was his domain. What he wanted to do was move the world into the church; and he would ultimately succeed, not at Pergamos, indeed, but at Rome.

For the present, however, he had to make do with persecution. He launched ten distinct onslaughts on the church, led by ten Caesars from Nero to Diocletian. The whole savage scheme failed. The day would come when he would replace all these persecuting Caesars with one persuasive patronizing Caesar. Diocletian would be replaced by Constantine, and the world would move into the church. And Satan's seat would be moved in with it.

But all that would be later. For now the postman from Patmos, when he arrived at Pergamos, at once felt the pressure of the atmosphere. Satan's seat was somewhere in that city. Pergamos was a dark, depressing, dangerous place to be.

Once he was inside the church at Pergamos, two things became apparent to him. First were the FAITHFUL DISCIPLES at Pergamos. They upheld the name of the Lord Jesus. That was the secret of their power, a power Satan well understood and feared. For Satan fears the name of Jesus. It is the saving name: "Whosoever shall call upon the name of the Lord shall be saved!" (Rom.10:13). It is the sanctifying name; we are to do all in the name of the Lord Jesus (Col.3:17). It is the sovereign name, for, at that name, every knee will one day bow (Phil.2:9-11). Behind that name is all the power and authority of the Godhead. And Satan is no match for God, as he very well knows.

So the faithful disciples at Pergamos held high the banner of Christ. And Satan, for all his throne and all his threats and all his throngs of fallen angels and demons could do little about it. Indeed he could do nothing at all apart from permission from a higher throne than his. He had already tried persecution. One disciples we know of, Antipas by name, had been slain. Very likely the disciples at Pergamos would have taken the postman to the very place where the martyrdom took place. They would point out the blood stains. They would take him to the tomb and vow their loyalty to the Lord afresh.

But there was a darker side. For there was FALSE DOCTRINE at Pergamos. The Lord bluntly calls it "the doctrine of Balaam" and it was more deadly than faggot and fire, scaffold and sword. For Satan had succeeded in getting some of his men accepted as Christians by the unwary believers at Pergamos.

The Old Testament "doctrine of Balaam" mentioned here, refers to the advice Balaam, a psychic of repute, gave to King Balak of Moab, as recorded in Numbers 24:25-25:1-3. After four futile attempts to curse God's people, a people God had blessed, Balaam said to the king: "You cannot curse them, my Lord King, so I suggest that you corrupt them. You cannot conquer them with the men of Moab no matter how many or how mighty they be. So try the women of Moab." That attempt to seduce God's people had succeeded only too well.

Now Satan was trying the same old trick again. The infiltration of the church by unbelievers had begun, and infidelity started to raise its head. The result was that there were some in the church who advocated a more liberal approach to things—toleration for extra-marital affairs, toleration for extra-biblical doctrines, and especially toleration for those who still had fellowship with idols. The champions of idolatry would maintain that idols were only visual aids to worship just as Catholics do today. The Lord, however, was outraged. "Repent!" He said, "or else!" If they would not act, HE would. Already the sword had been drawn. It was repent, or Else! It still is.

THE POSTMAN FROM PATMOS AT THYATIRA
REVELATIN 2:18-29

When the postman from Patmos arrived at the church at Thyatira, he met "that woman Jezebel," as the Holy Spirit calls her. It has been suggested that she was the wife of the pastor, or the presiding elder. She was certainly the driving force and inspiring genius of the church, whoever she was.

There was, of course, an Old Testament Jezebel, a woman of pagan convictions who was the doom and downfall of her husband and the curse of Israel and Judah (1 Kings 16:30-33). Her husband was putty in her hands. She it was who mobilized the secular arm to persecute the true people of God. And she it was who promoted, with all the power of the throne, idolatry and gross immorality to replace the true faith in Israel.

The New Testament Jezebel was her counterpart in the church. The Old Testament Jezebel, knew how to make herself attractive and knew, likewise, how to turn on the charm. She was clever, persuasive and vindictive. Her counterpart in the church at Thyatira doubtless was the same.

The postman doubtless took note of her BOASTFUL TITLE. She called herself "a prophetess." By the time the New Testament Jezebel seized the pulpit at Thyatira, the New Testament gift of prophecy was over. John was already writing the Bible's last book. So her claim was false. She called herself a prophetess, the Holy Spirit declared. What she preached was false. Her doctrine came from Satan, not from God.

We know something about her BRAZEN TEACHING. She was openly advocated a permissive attitude towards sexual sin and encouraged a liberal attitude towards idolatry and pagan festivals. In those days of the church (as in churches in pagan lands today), both immorality and idolatry were part of many believers' backgrounds. They had "turned to God from idols" (1 Thess.1:9-10). What kind of a spineless or godless kind of man was this woman's husband? Someone as weak and willful as Ahab of old, no doubt, the wishy-washy husband of the Old Testament Jezebel. And what about the other leaders of the church. What kind of men were they to put up with such teaching? Such was the fatal fascination of this woman, however, that even the Lord's servants were being seduced by her. It was not merely that this wicked woman smiled when profession believers had a lapse and fell into immorality and idolatry. She actively taught people to have fellowship with paganism and claimed prophetic authority for doing so. She was demon inspired.

And it went on. Little did she know, however, that she was living on BORROWED TIME. God was patient. He gave her time to repent. His love is such that it even embrace people like Jezebel and Judas. It never occurred to this New Testament Jezebel that the only reason God had not already acted in judgment was because He had pity for her lost soul and would rather see her repent than send retribution.

Then came the BITTER TORMENT. The sandglass of God's patience ran out. "I will cast her into a bed," God said. It was to be a bed of torment, a bed of some dreadful disease, perhaps where she would toss and turn in pain. Her punishment would be commensurate with the crime.

And her children, those who had embraced her doctrines and who had become ten thousand times more the children of hell than herself, they would share in her doom. But that had not yet happened when the postman passed that way. Jezebel of Thyatira would doubtless have liked to lay her hands on the letter he brought and torn it to shreds. The faithful postman saw to it that it fell into the hands of the faithful ones in the church. Not just the church local, the church at Thyatira, but the church universal would need that letter, too, when Jezebel's apostasy came to full flower at Rome.

THE POSTMAN FROM PATMOS AT SARDIS
REVELATION 3:1-6

The postman from Patmos had been hearing about this church from the moment he arrived in Asia Minor. It had made a name for itself. It was a church with a REPUTATION. That was the first thing of note about this church. It was known far and wide as a live church. Great must have been the disappointment of the postman, therefore, when he discovered that the church was dead. And that even what was still valid was in danger of dying as well. "A name, but dead!" So the Savior summed up the situation at Sardis.

There are stars in space, billions of light years away, which seem to be shining brightly but which, in reality, are actually dead. They are dark now, but their light still reaches us and will do so for ages still to come. They are shining solely by the light of a brilliant past. So it was at Sardis. Once it had been alive, shining brightly in its corner of the world. But no more! Now all it had was a reputation. The majority of its members were taken up with personalities, programs and politics. Outwardly all was well. It seemed to have a viable testimony. People in faraway places talked about it enthusiastically. But it was all hollow, a reputation that was all.

But then there was its REMNANT. They, too, had a name—"Thou hast a few <u>names</u> even in Sardis which have not defiled their garments," Jesus said. Doubtless the postman from Patmos met some of these, but they were a despised minority in the church. The new leadership wanted rid of them we can be sure. They were labeled as obscurantists, as obstructionists, as old-fashioned, as old fogies. They were a nuisance, always voting against the new policies and the new programs, always calling for a return to the Book, to the basics, to the early beginnings.

All John's sympathies were with these. He had been there, back at the beginning, when Jesus lived on earth. He had been there when the church was born with a rush and a roar in an upper room in far-off Jerusalem. He had been there when the power of the Holy Spirit reigned supreme. All John's writings had that in mind. He, the last living charter member of the church, a survivor from the first generation, wrote with passion to this compromising third generation. John's sympathies would all be with the remnant at Sardis. Probably it had been his banishment which had made it possible for the modern majority to move in.

But there was something else at Sardis. There was a RECKONING. The Lord issued a barely veiled threat—the dread possibility of names (we are back to names again) being blotted out.

One of two things happens to us in this life, either our sins get blotted out (Isa.44:22) or our names get blotted out. When sins are blotted out, God remembers them no more (Heb.8:12;10:17). So it is when names are blotted out. The ultimate horror of a lost eternity will be to realize that God Himself no longer remembers the names of those who are there. The threat of such a horrifying doom hovers like a ghost in the background of this dire warning.

Which brings me to the Lord's last word to this church with the big, empty name: "He that hath an ear, let him hear." This was the last call to this disappointing church, the last call to those who were all pretense.

THE POSTMAN FROM PATMOS AT PHILADELPHIA

REELATION 3:7-13

The postman from Patmos had now visited five of the seven churches to which special letters had been sent by the Lord. It had not been altogether a joyous experience. Though the church on earth was still young, it had long since left its first love. There was failure everywhere. Thyatira had been the worst, though Sardis, big boastful and bankrupt, as not far behind. Dead! As he set his face towards Philadelphia, he must have steeled his heart for more of the same. Was it to be another deluded church? Another debauched church? Another dead church?

But he was in for a pleasant surprise. For the church at Philadelphia was different. It was experiencing a three-fold revival. It was living proof that Christ was still building His church, and the gates of Hell could not prevail against it.

First it was experiencing an EVANGELICAL revival. The Lord had set before this church an open door, and no man could shut it. It had rediscovered gospel truth. Though that church was weak, and had but a little strength, it was making the gospel message heard at home and abroad. And doubtless people were being saved. The Devil was doing his best to cow the Christians and close the door; but the One Who had the key of David, the King of Glory Himself, was the One Who closed and opened doors, not Satan.

He has the key to every situation. The more the Devil tries to slam doors which the Lord was opened, the more he jams his fingers.

Then, too, there was an ECCLESIASTICAL revival. The background of this revival was the synagogue of Satan. What had been conceded by the church at Smyrna was confronted by the church at Philadelphia. The believers at Philadelphia had rediscovered church truth. The "synagogue of Satan" was made up of people who confused Judaism with Christianity. They did not rightly divide the Word of Truth. The church is not spiritual Israel. Christianity and Judaism are incompatible. Christ is the end of the Law for righteousness. For Gentiles in the church to say they were Jews was a violation of truth. They had forgotten Paul's letter to the Ephesians, a circular letter well-known in Asia Minor and read no doubt and copied and kept by all the churches of Roman Asia. The letter dealt specifically with the mystery of the church, an entity quite distinct from the Nation of Israel. The Philadelphis believers took up the challenge; and with what little strength they had, they confronted the synagogue of Satan cultists. The Lord promised them victory.

Finally, there was an ESCHATOLOGICAL revival. The church had rediscovered truth concerning the second coming of Christ. They had rediscovered the blessed hop of the church, the truth that the Lord's coming would be pre-tribulational. The promise was clear. "I will keep thee from the hour of trial which shall come upon all the world . . ." The Lord was not referring to some local trial, or to some persecution confined to the Roman world. The reference is to the Great Tribulation mentioned frequently in Scripture (Matt.24:20-22). Along with the rediscovery of this blessed hope, that the true church would escape of the Great Tribulation, was a fresh understanding of the judgment seat of Christ. "Let no man take thy crown!" the believers are warned.

The church was small. Its strength was small. But mighty was its recovery of fundamental truth. The postman must have left for Laodicea with a fresh spring in his step and a fresh song in his soul.

THE POSTMAN FROM PATMOS
AT LAODICEA
REVELATION 3:14-22

The postman from Patmos had no trouble at all, we can be sure, in finding the church of the Laodiceans. Everybody who was anybody either went there or had friends or relatives who did.

In the first place, it was WEALTHY. The Bible says it was "rich and increased in goods and had need of nothing." It had, by far, the best paying pulpit in the Province. Money was never a problem at Laodicea. It had money enough and to spare. Consequently, it did not need the Holy Ghost. It could buy talent just as it could buy anything else. It could buy buildings and beautiful furniture. Like the rich fool of the Lord's parable, who planned on building bigger and better barns, the church at Laodicea was rich and increased in goods. It went in for bigger and better buildings. It did not realize that its balance sheet in heaven, like that of the rich fool, was marked "Bankrupt!" For the church of the Laodiceans (note how the Lord addresses it) was a well-run, superbly managed business—big business, too. So it could buy talent—the most polished and eloquent preacher in the Province, the most talented and accomplished preacher in the Province, the most talented and accomplished choir members, the most efficient and organized staff, the most professional counselors and pastors, the most enticing programs. It was rich. It had need of nothing.

And it was WORLDLY. It was a society church. The upper crust of the city had their membership there. Politicians went there, for votes. Corporate executives went there, to make contacts. Intellectuals went there, to debate. Nobody had to be saved or baptized or believe anything in particular to belong. The most sought after commendation for membership was to be somebody in society.

It was WARNED. The Lord was not impressed by the wealthy and worldly wisdom of this church. It was lukewarm—that was His own word for it. It was neither hot nor cold, neither one thing nor the other, neither Christian nor pagan. Lukewarmness is the condition of a liquid when it is reduced to room temperature. Put two containers on a table, one containing boiling hot water and the other containing freezing cold water. In time, both will settle their differences by becoming conformed to room temperature. Such was the church of Laodicea. It had so accommodated itself to the temperature of the world that the Lord said it made Him sick. It was wretched and poor and blind and miserable and naked, He declared. Worse! It didn't know it.

The Laodicean church reminds us of the Emperor, of whom the children's story tells, and of his new clothes. Some itinerant tailors, you remember, had offered to make him a wardrobe of invisible clothes. When he went out in his new, invisible garments, everyone else could see he was naked; but he imagined himself to be gloriously arrayed in invisible finery. Such was the church of the Laodiceans. It strutted proudly on the world stage. The watching angels saw that it was naked.

Finally, it was WICKED. The Lord wanted no part of it. He was outside the whole thing. He had nothing to say to it or its leaders. He addressed His appeal to individuals here and there: "Behold, I stand at the door, and knock" He said, "if any man hear my voice, and open the door, I will come in to him, and will sup with him, and he with me." The postman delivered his letter and went on his way.

The last thing he saw as, his task over, he walked on out of history, was the Lord of Glory shut out of His own church.

THE FOUR AND TWENTY ELDERS

REVELATION 4-5

Amidst scenes of glory that virtually defy description, John contemplates the four and twenty elders. These are the crowned royalties of heaven, angelic beings of high dignity and destiny. They are mentioned seven times in the apocalypse. They seem to be members of a heavenly priesthood, the priesthood which seems to have inspired David to arrange Israel's Temple priesthood into twenty-four groups. Almost every time we see these celestial elders, they are off their thrones and down on their faces in worship before God.

We first see them in the company of the cherubim. As the voices of the cherubim awake the echoes of the everlasting hills ("Holy!" "Holy!" "Holy!"), these elders respond. Down on their faces they go! And there go their crowns, cast at Jesus' feet. They lift their voices. They say to the Lord of Glory: "Thou art worthy for Thou hast created all things" (Rev.4:11).

Presently the Lamb of Calvary is unveiled in heaven, as the only One fit govern the globe. The seven-sealed scroll, the title deed of earth is given to Him. Down the elders go again! And there go their crowns as the chanting cherubim proclaim the goodness and glory of God. "Thou art worthy for Thou wast slain," is the song the elders sing. (Rev.9-11)

Now all creatures great and small are called upon to pay tribute to the Lamb. From the high halls of heaven they come; from the dark and dreadful dungeons of the damned; up from the deepest depths of the sea; drawn from the utmost bounds of the everlasting hills. Every knee must bow. Every tongue must confess that Jesus Christ is Lord. Down fall the four and twenty elders once again, overwhelmed, thrilled to the core of their being to see the Lamb of God coming into His own at long last (Rev.5:14).

And, once again, the scene is changed. All hell has been let loose on earth. The Antichrist's gestapo are hunting down all Jews, and also all Gentiles converted by the preaching of the 144,000 witnesses. A countless multitude is martyred and are received into Glory. As these triumphant saints go marching in the heavenly hosts, the countless angels who surround the elders and the cherubim and the throne of God in Glory, fall down on their faces and worship God (Rev.7:11-17).

Now it is the turn of God's two witnesses (possibly Enoch and Elijah sent back to earth). Long and fierce has been their battle with the Beast in and around Jerusalem, his religious capital. In the end he slays them. God then raises them and raptures them and shakes Jerusalem to its foundations with an earthquake. As these glorious two come marching into Glory midst the cheers of the angelic hosts, and as the angel sounds the seventh and final trumpet, down go the Elders again, worshipping on their faces before God (Rev.11:11-18).

The two witnesses are followed into heaven by the 144,000 witnesses. These fiery evangelists have marched unscathed into every capital of the world, winning converts everywhere. They are given a special rapture into heaven. They sing a new song, standing before the throne of God. The four and twenty elders are enthralled, so enthralled, in fact, they forget to fall on their faces before God! (Rev.14:1-5).

And now the time has come for great Babylon, the glittering commercial capital of the Antichrist, the sin showcase of the world, to be judged. Great, sudden and absolute is its fall. Again the four and twenty elders respond. Down on their faces they go. "Amen! Allelujah," they say (Rev.18:1-19:6).

And that's the last we see of them. Their thrones are now to be vacated. Their place in heaven will be taken the church-age overcomes who will come into their own at last, and who will sit enthroned, higher than them all, as co-heirs of Glory with the Lamb.

THE LORD SHALL DESCEND FROM HEAVEN

I THESSALONIANS 4:13-18

The shout will shatter the age-long silence of the Godhead. It is a silence which began with the triumphant shout of the dying Christ on the cross at Calvary. It has lasted already for nearly two thousand years. It has been silence long, prolonged and absolute; a silence which has caused scoffers to blaspheme and saints to stumble. But what other answer could God give to the crime of Calvary? It was either silence or wrath. God chose silence. But the silence will be broken one of these days. The Church will be gone up with a shout and wrath will come down with a roar. It will be rapture for the Church and wrath for the world.

First, there are THE SOUNDS. It will all begin with "a shout": "the Lord shall descend from heaven with a shout," Paul says. Only three times in the Bible does Jesus shout. He shouted at the tomb of Lazarus, and a dead man came to life. He shouted on the cross; and many bodies of the saints which slept, arose and came out of their graves after His resurrection and went into the Holy City and appeared unto many (Matt.27:50:52-53). He will shout at the time of His coming again, and a whole Church will rise—a multitude that no man can number. The shout is for the Church.

It will be accompanied by the voice of the archangel. The voice of the archangel is for the angels, to summon the angels for war. The rapture of the Church will mean that the amnesty is over. The nationals of heaven are taken home, and God will declare war on a world which murdered His Son. The angels come into their own. They appear in chapter after chapter of the Apocalypse.

Then, too, there will be the trump of God. The trump of God is for Israel. The fact that the nation of Israel has been reborn and is back in the land tells us that end time events are upon us. The time of Jacob's trouble cannot be too far off. These are the sounds—the shout, the voice, the trump.

Then there are THE SIGHTS. There are two of them. The first is the resurrection of all those who have died in Christ. "The dead in Christ shall rise first," Paul says, those whose names are written in the Lamb's book of life. They hoped against hope that the Lord would come in their lifetime, but death came instead. However, they will rise. The resurrection of Christ is the guarantee of that. They will come bounding from their tombs shouting, "O grave, where is thy victor?' (1 Cor.15:55).

Then comes the rapture of all those who are alive and remain when Jesus comes for His Church. They will leap into the sky, changed, transformed in a moment, the twinkling of an eye. As they soar upwards to the courts of bliss, they will cry: "O death, where is thy sting?" And one and all, the living saints and those who once were dead, will become just like Jesus; and their bodies will be just like His.

And then there will be THE SONGS. There will be a song of comfort in the gloom: "Comfort one another with these words," Paul says. The Christians at Thessalonica had lost some of their number to death, and they thought they had lost them forever. Paul's letter was intended to comfort them, and also believers in all the ages yet to come. The philosophers, scientists and cultists of the world have no comfort to offer when death moves in. Only the Gospel offers us the blessed hope of the coming again of One Who has the keys of death and hell (Rev.1:18).

And, finally, there will be the song of consummation in the Glory. With the Lord! With the Lord! What more could we want than that?

"He and I in that bright glory,
One glad joy shall share,
Mine to be forever with Him,
His that I am there."

I THESSOLONIANS
I THESSOLONIANS 1:8-10

Paul had barely founded the church at Thessalonica when he was forced to leave because of persecution. He left behind a church composed of babes in Christ. Paul made his way to Corinth; and from there, he wrote his first letter to these infant believers. To spur them on the growth and godliness, he wrote to them primarily of the second coming of Christ. Each of the five chapters in this epistle mentions it.

In chapter one he speaks of A COMING DAY: "Ye turned to God from idols . . . and to wait for His Son from heaven, even Jesus, which delivered us from the wrath to come." Waiting! The idea is best illustrated in the marriage customs of the Jews in Bible times. First came the betrothal. The prospective bridegroom left his father's house and came to where the awaiting bride lived. There he negotiated a marriage covenant and paid the purchase price. Once the price was paid, the covenant went into effect; and the couple was virtually regarded as man and wife and the bride was regarded as set apart for her groom. The betrothal was ratified by the bride and groom drinking from a cup of wine. All this Jesus has done for us already.

After establishing the marriage covenant, the groom returned home where He remained for a year. During this time, both bride and groom prepared for the coming wedding. At length the day came, and the bridegroom came to take his bride to live with him. The bride expected him but did not know the exact time of his arrival. His coming was announced by a shout.

Next, Paul speaks of A CORONATION DAY: "For what is our hope, or joy, or crown of rejoicing? Ye! in the presence of our Lord Jesus Christ at His coming." Paul sees himself at the judgment seat of Christ, overwhelmed with bliss as he sees his beloved converts beaming at him in Glory. They are the guarantee of his crown.

Then he tells them of A CONFIRMATION DAY: "To the end that ye may be established, unblameable, in holiness before God even our Father at the coming of our Lord Jesus Christ with all his saints." The Holy Spirit is already at work in our hearts, seeking to make us more like Jesus. The work will be completed, in a flash, when Jesus comes. "We shall be like Him for we shall see Him as He is," John says. We shall take our place with all His saints at His coming. That will be the confirmation of the glorious fact that we belong to Him.

For up ahead is a CONSUMMATION DAY: "The Lord Himself shall descend from heaven with a shout . . . the dead in Christ shall rise first, then we which are alive and remain shall be caught up to meet the Lord in the air. So shall we ever be with the Lord." Let us continue the analogy of a Jewish wedding. The arrival of the bride was heralded with a shout. The groom received his bride; and the couple, with their companions, returned to his father's house. Just so, the Lord receives His Church and takes her to Glory. By the time the Jewish bride and groom are thus escorted home, the wedding guests are all assembled. The bride, heavily veiled, in the company of the groom, is escorted to the bridal chamber. They retire into seclusion. Once the consummation is announced, the feast begins and lasts for seven days.

Likewise we shall arrive home. The Old Testament saints will be gathered to welcome us home. The Old Testament saints will be gathered to welcome us home. The spiritual union of Christ and His Church will be proclaimed. The marriage supper will take place in heaven while the final seven-year period of trouble and tribulation works out its course on earth.

MY FATHER'S HOUSE

JOHN 14:1-6

"I'm going back home!" Jesus said. The disciples were stunned. Ever since His unveiling on the mount of transfiguration, He had been preparing them for the news; but, even so, it was like a bombshell. He sat down and sought to comfort them. We look first at their BROKEN HEARTS. "Let not your heart be troubled," He said. The word for "troubled" here is the same word used of the reaction of the disciples sometime before, when they saw Him walking towards them over a wild and stormy sea. They thought He was a ghost. They were "troubled," agitated. But it was Jesus! He stilled the storm and landed them safe on the distant shore. As then, so now! All was well. He'd see them safely home. In the meantime His promise is sure. "I will not leave you orphans." He said.

Now let us look at their BETTER HOME. When the Queen of Sheba saw the glory of Solomon, including the golden temple and his own magnificent palace, she was overwhelmed. "The half was never told me," she said. We, too, will be awed by the indescribable glory of our home on high. He, the great Carpenter of Nazareth, has been working on that place now for nigh on two thousand years.

"I go to prepare a <u>place</u> for you," He said. The word for "place" is of interest. It is <u>topos</u> which gives us our English word for topography. It suggests a geographical, topographical location. It reinforces the fact that He is preparing a real place for real people.

"I go to prepare a place for <u>you</u>," He said. This place is not a home for the heavenly hosts on high. They already have their own estate. This place is for <u>us</u>. How Satan must gnash his teeth in rage as he catches glimpses of the ivory palaces, the Edenic parks, the countless wonders of that glorious place the Son of God is preparing for <u>us</u>! And, adding bitterness to that pill he is forced to swallow, is the fact that he is powerless to wreck and ruin that world the way he has wrecked and ruined this one.

But we can take yet another look: "I will come again and receive you unto myself that where I am there may ye be also." Which points us to our <u>**BLESSED HOPE**</u>. Just as He came to earth the first time to literally fulfill all the promises that had to do with His coming to redeem, so He will come back again to literally fulfill all the promises that have to do with His coming to reign. There is more in the Bible about His coming again than about any other theme. It is mentioned 1,845 times in the Old Testament and 318 times in the New. It is found in 27 of the 39 Old Testament books and in 17 of the 27 New Testament books.

"I'm coming!" He says. As the old hymn puts it:

"Midst the darkness, storm and sorrow
One bright gleam I see,
Well I know the blessed morrow
Christ will come for me.

He, Who in the hour of sorrow,
Bore the curse alone,
I, who in the lonely desert
Trod where He had gone.

He and I in that bright glory
One deep joy shall share;
Mine to be forever with Him,
His that I am there."

THE DAYS OF NOAH

MATTHEW 24

Jesus said that the last days, prior to His coming again, would be just like the days of Noah. Those days, described in Genesis 4-6, reveal seven characteristics of the days of Noah which are also characteristics of our own day and age. First, they were days of SPIRITUAL DECLINE. The faith which had been delivered to Adam, for which the martyr Abel was prepared to shed his blood, and which had been distorted by Cain into a false religion, that faith had largely disappeared in Noah's day. Those who knew the true and living God were becoming an ever-increasing minority in this world (Gen.7:1).

The days of Noah were not only days of spiritual decline, they were also days of SOCIAL DILEMMA. This was marked by a population explosion ("men began to multiply"), and by a corresponding increase in crime. God put man in a garden. Cain put him in a city (Gen.4:17). And the great cities of the world, bursting with people, became jungles of crime. "The earth," God says, "was filled with violence" (Gen.6:11).

Then, too, the days of Noah were days of SHAMELESS DEPRAVITY. There was polygamy, for instance. God's laws for marriage were set aside (Gen.4:19). And there was pornography for "every imagination of man was only evil continually" (Gen.6:5,11).

Next, the days of Noah were days of SCIENTIFIC DEVELOPMENT. Tremendous strides were being taken in science, technology and engineering. The ark, believed to be as big as some of our modern ocean-going liners, was built by Noah and his helpers. The engineers of that day had the necessary skills to build a vessel which was to face the most terrible storm ever known (Gen.4:22).

Moreover, the days of Noah were days of STRONG DELUSION. In commenting on the days of Noah, Jesus passed over the wickedness of that age and underlined the ignorance of coming judgment which characterized the antediluvians, and that despite the fact that Noah had been preaching it for years. "They knew not," Jesus said, "until the Flood came and took them all away" (Matt.24:37-39). They were blinded by their secular humanism, materialism and new-age occultism.

Then, too, the days of Noah were days of SOME DEVOTION. For God never leaves Himself without a witness. The more degenerate the times, the more definite the testimony, both in terms of faithful preaching on the one hand and fulfilled prophesy on the other hand. Noah was a preacher, and Enoch (2 Pet.2:5: Jude 14-15) was a prophet. A sample of his actual preaching is preserved in the book of Jude. Both bore witness to coming judgment. Enoch gave a prophetic name to his son, Methuselah— it means, "When he dies it (the Flood) shall come" (Gen.5:21). The death of Methuselah, incidentally, took place in the first month of the Flood year.

Finally, the days of Noah were days of SUDDEN DESTRUCTION. "My Spirit shall not always strive with man," God said (Gen.6:3). A date was set in heaven for the Flood to begin. When it came, in all its fury, chaos descended on the planet. Only eight people were saved—those who had believed God and accepted the invitation to take refuge in the Ark. They were all members of Noah's family.

These features of Noah's day are all characteristics of our day. We live in a world in which evil men and seducers are waxing worse and worse, a world ripening fast for judgment. "What manner of people ought we to be," Peter says.

THE RIVER
EZEKIEL 47:1-12

The scene is millennial. Its scope is monumental. Ezekiel's closing end time visions are focused on the awesome temple yet to grace the earth in days, soon to be, when Jesus will reign "from the river to the ends of the world" (Ps.72:8). It is the river that thrills him here. It flows out from the temple, and it brings life and loveliness everywhere it goes. Obviously, however, there must be more to it than that. And so there is.

In the Bible, God the Father is likened to a <u>fountain</u> of living water (Jer.2:15). God the Son is likened to a <u>well</u> of living water (Jno.4:14), and God the Holy spirit is likened to a <u>river</u> of living water (Jno.7:37-39).

On the eighth day of the Feast of Tabernacles, something special happened. To begin with, the day itself was always a Sunday. It was kept as a special Sabbath and it was the great, climactic conclusion of all the festivities of the year. The priests brought vessels of water from the pool of Siloam and poured it in a river over the steps of the temple. Jesus seized upon this activity to introduce His people to the Holy Spirit Who was soon to replace Him on earth as resident member of the Godhead.

Coming back now, to the end-time river Ezekiel saw coming out of the future millennial temple, there are four things we can learn about the river of the Spirit. Note, first, <u>the general direction of the river</u>. The prophet stepped into this life-giving stream until the water was to his ankles. His walk was now controlled by the river. Where it went, he went. He followed its leading, treading a path of obedience. It was the path that Jesus trod from the virgin womb of Mary in Bethlehem to the virgin tomb of Joseph in Jerusalem. It is that path of obedience we must tread if we would know more of the Spirit of God.

We note, also, <u>the growing dominance of the river</u>. The prophet walked out a thousand cubits deeper into the river. The water was now to his knees. The knees remind us of <u>submission</u>—"Every knee shall bow," Paul says (Phil.2:10-11)—and they remind us of <u>supplication</u> for we bend our knees when we pray. Water to the knees brings us into deeper experience of the Holy Spirit. How little we know about praying in the Holy Spirit. "We know not what to pray for as we ought" Paul says (Rom.8:26-27). The Holy Spirit must help our infirmities in this regard.

We note, next, <u>the great dynamic of the river</u>. Another thousand cubits into the river, and the water reaches to the loins. The full force of the river can now be felt. In Scripture the loins refer to the lower part of the back, the pivot of the whole body. The loins also refer to the seat of generative power, the seat of life. To have one's "loins girt" in the Bible means to be ready for vigorous effort. Water to the loins takes us to an even deeper knowledge of the Holy Spirit as the One Who provides power for service and for bringing people to the birth.

Finally, we note the glorious design of the river. Another thousand cubits into the river and the prophet is in deep water—"waters to swim in." When we swim we surrender ourselves wholly to the water. Our feet no longer cleave to the earth. Our whole body is at the disposal of the flowing stream. Moreover, when a person is swimming, all that can be seen of him is his head. <u>That</u> is the glorious design of the Holy Spirit—that we should be so submerged in His will that all that can be seen is Jesus, our Head. We are thus borne along by the Spirit, buoyed up by the Spirit and blessed of the Spirit of God. The result will be cleansing and fruitfulness everywhere.

THE MAN OF SIN
II THESSALONIANS 2:3-12

There had been some kind of spirit utterance in the infant church at Thessalonica. Someone had spoken with a lying "tongue." In addition, there had been a "voice of prophesy;" but it had not been the Holy Spirit's voice. Like the infant church's gift of "tongues," its gift of prophecy could also be imitated by a lying spirit. The Thessalonians were far too ready to take such manifestations as of God without testing the spirits to make sure that the communication had come from God.

In those days, before the completion of the New Testament canon of Scripture, tongues and prophecy were still valid gifts. If caution was necessary in those days, how much more skeptical we should be in these days when these foundational gifts have been withdrawn. (1 Cor.13:8; 1 John 4:1-3).

That was not all. There had also been a forged letter purporting to have come from Paul. Thus the deception was three-fold (a lying tongue, a false prophesy and a forged letter), and a three-fold cord is not easily broken. The Bereans would not have been so gullible. We read that they were "more noble than those in Thessalonica, in that they received the word with all readiness of mind and searched the Scriptures daily whether those things were so" (Acts 17:11).

Paul took advantage of this deception in the Thessalonian church to unveil a larger deception—Satan's most secret plans for the end times. We have, first, THE UNVEILING OF SATAN'S MAN: "Let no man deceive you by any means," says Paul, using a double negative to reinforce the warning. He tells us that before the man of sin can be revealed, there has to be "a falling away first," and overwhelming apostasy. Satan's man is called "the man of sin" and also "the son of perdition." We generally recognize this prodigy of wickedness as the antichrist. He is called "the Beast" in the Apocalypse. He is "the little horn" of Daniel 7, the final Gentile world ruler. He is supported by an apostate Jew, called "the false prophet" (Rev.13). The Antichrist will be killed but will come back to life again (Rev.17:8). In his early career, he is called "the beast out of the sea" (Rev.13:1) but, in his later career, he is "the beast out of the Abyss" (Rev.7:8-14).

Paul tells the Thessalonians that the Holy Spirit, working through the Church, is at work in the world today, holding back the rising tides of wickedness. In the end, however, the godless forces working in society will produce the man of sin, once the Holy Spirit no longer restrains them. The rapture of the Church will make it possible for Satan to bring in his man. "<u>Then</u> shall that wicked (one) be revealed," Paul says.

Immediately after the rapture, there will not only be a sudden acceleration in every kind of wickedness; but chaos will descend upon the world (Rev.6). The Devil will then produce his man. He will revive the old Roman Empire, sweep away all opposition and take control of the whole world. "Who can make war with beast?" (Rev.13:4) the hesitant nations will say, as they sign up as members of the new global empire.

Once global power is in his hands, the Antichrist will force people to receive his mark and worship his image. He will then launch a global persecution of the Jews and all who hold the Judeo-Christian ethnic. In the end, God's judgments will weaken the Antichrist. The nations of the east will rebel and mobilize against him and will march westward, setting the state for Armageddon and the return of Christ to reign.

Paul warns the Thessalonians against unbelief. Unbelievers left behind at the rapture of the Church, people who have heard the Gospel and rejected it, will believe the Devil's lies. Indeed God Himself will withdraw Himself from all those who choose the lie over His Son, He Who is the Truth (Jno.14:6). It is always that way. People who disbelieve or ignore the Truth lay themselves open to believe a Lie. It is always so. Let the unbeliever beware.

JESUS IS COMING AGAIN
MATTHEW 24

Four things about the second coming of Christ should fill our souls with joy.

First, HE IS COMING SWIFTLY (Matt.24:27): "As the lightening cometh out of the east and shineth even unto the west, so shall the coming of the Son of man be." Once He steps into the sky, there will be no time to get right with God, no time to make amends. Swift as fast-paced lightning He will come. Lightning is incredibly swift. A spark from a cloud to the earth can measure as much as eight miles and can travel at the speed of 100 million feet per second. Lightning that reaches from cloud to cloud can be twenty to 100 miles long. The Lord Jesus is coming at the speed of a lightning flash. It will be "in a moment," it will be "in the twinkling of an eye." Happy moment for His own! Horrendous moment for His foes!

Lightning can be deadly. Sheet lightning has no particular form, it is just a bright flash in the sky, but forked lightning comes charged with 15 million volts of electrical power. Jesus is coming like that, swiftly and in power.

Then, too, HE IS COMING SOLEMNLY (Matt.24:37-39): "As in the days before the Flood they were eating and drinking, marrying and giving in marriage until the Flood came and took them all away, so shall the coming of the Son of man be." The Flood years were similar to the days in which we live. In Noah's day the true faith was rapidly disappearing and pornographic society, one filled with violence, took its place. Men were making tremendous strides in the fields of science, commerce and entertainment. Permissiveness was the popular attitude of a lawless society which allowed the guilty to go unpunished and which endorsed all kinds of deviant behavior. The majority of people were ignorant of God's Word. "They knew not," Jesus said in His commentary on these things (Matt.24:39). People were clever enough when it came to material things, but they were wholly blind to spiritual things. They ignored the signs which pointed to coming doom. They "knew not" until it was too late. So it was then. So it is today.

Then, too, HE IS COMING SECRETLY Matt.24:42-43): "Watch therefore for ye know not what hour your lord doth come." This aspect of the Lord's second coming has to do with the <u>rapture</u>, not with the final return of the Lord to reign. The date of the final return will be known to those who believe. It will be exactly 1260 days from the day the Antichrist seizes the rebuilt Jewish Temple and begins the Great Tribulation to the day of Christ's return to reign (Rev.12:6). Before that happens, the Lord is coming like a Thief, coming secretly, when least expected, to snatch away His own people. "Of <u>that</u> day and hour knoweth no man," Jesus said (Mk.13:32). In Matthew's account of this secret event the Lord goes on to actually describe the rapture of the Church (Matt.4:36, 40-44). "Be ready!" That's the word!

Finally, HE IS COMING SURELY (Matt.25:6): Like the Bridegroom. "Behold the Bridegroom cometh; go ye out to meet Him," will be the cry. Now we are invited to view the second coming from His point of view. A Bridegroom! What a picture of eager anticipation! He has been gone for a long time. But He has been busy preparing a place for us, a home beyond the sky. His Spirit has been here in His stead, however, and has been busy calling out a people for His Name. But one of these days, He will come. And we'll be gone! What a day of rejoicing that will be.

PETER AND THE BOMB
II PETER 3:10-13

The atomic age burst upon the world with a rush and a roar at 8:15 in the morning on August 16, 1945, when the United States dropped the first atomic bomb on Hiroshima. The bomb exploded 1800 feet above the city, and the city of some 350,000 was virtually leveled. Man now had an apocalyptic weapon of mass destruction in his hands.

It is an extraordinary fact that Simon Peter, an uneducated Galilean peasant, wrote down an accurate description of the nuclear age two thousand years ago. The background of this astonishing prophecy is one of growing skepticism and scorn for the things of God, especially for truth concerning the second coming of Christ (2 Pet.3:4). Scoffers fail to reckon on the fact that God's timetable is much vaster than ours. A thousand years with Him passes as swiftly as a twenty-four day does with us.

Peter's prophecy, while not couched in scientific language, is amazingly accurate just the same. The Greek words he chooses are very precise words. "The heavens shall pass away with a great noise," he says, "the elements shall melt with fervent heat; the earth also and the works that are therein shall be burned up . . . all these things shall be dissolved . . ."

Let us begin with the word "elements." The English word comes from the Latin elementum, which, in turn, is a translation of the Greek word stoicheia, the word Peter uses here. Various meanings are attached to the word, including the idea of the betters of the alphabet, of a simple sound of speech, and also of the letters of the alphabet placed in order. It was used in the realm of physics to describe the components into which matter is divided. In today's English, we would use the word "atoms" to translate it. As the letters of the alphabet are the component parts of words, so atoms are the component parts of the elements and of matter.

The word for dissolve comes from luo—"to break up, destroy, melt." It is sometimes translated "unloose," as when John the Baptist said he was not worthy to "unloose" the latchet of Christ's shoe. The Lord used the word, also, after raising Lazarus. "Loose him," He said. Peter, using the available words of his day, foretold a coming great conflagration of the heavens and the earth implying that the elemental particles of matter (which we now call "atoms") will be dissolved, untied, released. Their energies, hitherto imprisoned, would be set free to cause a fearful holocaust.

The expression, "a great noise," comes from the word rhoizedon, found only here. W. E. Vine says the word signifies "a rushing sound as of roaring flames." The phrase, "fervent heat," comes from kausoo, a medical word noting a fever. Peter tells us when this will take place at the very end of time.

It is comforting to know that God will press that button, not man. The thousand year reign of Christ will come and go before this final conflagration described by Peter will place. Some minor nuclear activity may take place in the tribulation period (Rev.16:2), but the Church will be gone before then and God Himself will hold back the final nuclear woe until all His own, including His millennial hosts, are far beyond its reach.

WHAT A WAY TO BEGIN
REVELATION 1:4-5

The Book of Revelation begins with a burst of names which set forth the glory of the Lord Jesus. He is called Him which is, which was, which is to come. He is called Jesus Christ, the faithful witness, first begotten of the dead, Prince of the Kings of the earth. Names! For, after all, this book is "the revelation," the unveiling of Jesus Christ. Throughout the Old Testament period, God's principle way of revealing Himself was by means of His Names. There are three primary names for God . . . Elohim (El, Elah), Jehovah and Adonai (Adon). There are three compound names linked with El (El Shaddai, El Elyon and El Olam—Almighty God, God Most High and Everlasting God). And there are various compound names linked with Jehovah (Jehoval Elohim, Adonai Jehovah, Jehovah Sabath and so on Lord God, Lord God, Lord of Hosts, and so on). These names tell us much about God. Here, in the opening chapter of the Apocalypse, we catch five glimpses of our Lord in Glory, fresh revelations of Him by means of His names.

He is THE INFINITE ONE, "Him which is, and which was, and which is to come." He is the One Who transcends time. Past, Present and Future are all gathered up and put beneath His feet. What we actually have here is a paraphrase of the Old Testament name Jehovah. The name implies that God always was, always is and that He will always be.

He is THE INCARNATE ONE, "Jesus Christ." That is the Name He assumed when He came down here to live. Jesus reveals Him as the Man; Christ reveals Him as the Messiah. That was how John knew Him best. So very much a Man! Yet God, over all, blessed for ever. The One of Whom we sing:

> *"Fairest of all the earth beside,*
> *Dearest of all unto His bride,*
> *Fulness Divine in Thee I see,*
> *Beautiful Man of Calvary."*

He is that longed-for "Daysman" for whom Job sought, that one Mediator between God and man.

He is THE INERRANT ONE, the Faithful Witness. He is the One Who spoke for God with unfailing compassion, unerring comprehension, and unflinching courage. He spoke with authority, and not as the Scribes. He witnessed to the truth without fear or favor. He spoke in a particularly pungent way, conveying truth in a memorable, undiluted form. And He was never wrong. He never had to retract a single statement, never had to apologize for anything He said. Men's hearts were an open book to Him. Even His enemies said: "Never man spake like this Man."

He is THE INITIAL ONE, the First begotten of the dead. As J. B. Phillips puts it: "Life from nothing began through Him; life from the dead began through Him" (Col.1:15).

> *"Death could not hold its prey,*
> *He tore the bars away,*
> *Up from the grave He arose,*
> *With a mighty triumph o'er His foes."*

All others die, victims to the dread reaper's scythe. Even the half dozen raised by Elijah, Elisha and Jesus died again. He was the First begotten of the dead, the Pioneer of a new race of resurrected and raptured saints.

He is THE INVINCIBLE ONE, Prince of the kings of the earth. All earthly crowns will be case at His feet when He comes back to reign. His coming empire here on earth will last for a thousand years and it will stretch from the river to the ends of the earth" (Zech.9:10). Indeed:

> *"Jesus shall reign where're the sun*
> *Doth its successive journeys run*
> *His Kingdom stretch from shore to shore*
> *Till moons shall wax and wane no more."*

The rest of the book of Revelation is the outworking in history of these things.

GRACE BE UNTO YOU AND PEACE (1)

REVELATION 1:4-6

"Grace be unto you and peace" (Rev.1:4). Thus the Book of Revelation begins—more like a Pauline epistle than a great apocalypse. Here is a book which deals primarily with judgment, but God begins it with grace. In this book we see people getting what they do deserve—judgment after judgment from a God Who's patience is exhausted at last. The floodtides of His wrath which have been dammed back since Calvary are now released. The dams burst. The pent-up oceans of His holy anger against sin, and against the murder of His Son, pour out now in all their fury. But first, God speaks of His grace. God tells people that judgment is His strange work. He would far rather offer them His grace. Grace, as the word is used in Scripture, is the outpouring of God's unmerited kindness to the lost.

Years ago a reclaimed drunkard named Sam Duncannon used to haunt the halls of the Glasgow mission in Scotland. He was poor. He was simple, but he was saved. He collected pictures, and he collected poems. He would find a picture, paste it onto some cardboard, find a matching poem and past that alongside the picture. Then he would give these picture poems to the derelicts who came through the mission, hoping they might bring some brightness into their lives.

One day someone gave Sam Duncannon a picture of Niagara Falls. He loved it. He looked and looked for a poem to put beside it. But he could not find one.

Then one day D. L. Moody came to the Glasgow mission, along with Mr. Sankey. Mr. Sankey got up to sing; and, at once, Sam knew he had found the words he wanted for his picture of Niagara Falls. This is what Mr. Sankey sang:

> *"Have you on the Lord believed?*
> *Still there's more to follow;*
> *Of His grace have you received?*
> *Still there's more to follow,*
> *Oh the grace the Father shows,*

Still there's more to follow.
Freely He His grace bestows
Still there's more to follow —
More and more, and more and more,
Always more to follow;
Oh His matchless, boundless love
Still there's more to follow."

Such indeed is the boundless grace of God. "Grace be unto you!" Grace to defy the Devil to the very end! Grace to win souls from beneath the very throne of the Beast! Grace poured out upon the two witnesses and then superabundantly upon the 144,000 witnesses until the converts of the judgment age to come promise to outnumber all those of history.

And yet more grace! Grace to send an angel with "the everlasting gospel" to win still more souls before the bowls of wrath are outpoured (Rev.14:6-7). Indeed, so great is God's desire for lost people to be saved, right down to the last possible moment that He reduces the angel's message here to the lowest possible terms. Here is no elaborate New Testament theology. Here is no demand for good works of any kind. It is the primeval gospel, the simplest, most universal beliefs available to all men everywhere based on the evidence of creation and conscience (the kind of thing we have in Romans 1:18-20). "Fear God and give glory to Him, for the hour of His judgment is come, and worship Him that made heaven, and earth, and the sea, and the fountains of waters." There will be no time left to discuss the profound theology of the cross—besides the prerogative of preaching Christ and Him crucified is not given to angels but to men. But men alas have failed. With judgment fires already poised on high and about the descend there are still untold millions still untold, so an angel is sent. He calls for the barest essentials of belief God can accept; and one last, burning call is given from heaven. Such is our God—a God of matchless grace.

GRACE BE UNTO YOU AND PEACE (2)

REVELATION 1:4-6

"Grace be unto you . . . and peace! Imagine that! What a way to begin the Apocalypse, especially when the book of Revelation deals with the very opposite of peace. Its themes are those of bloodshed and war. It rings with the din and noise of strife. It tells of carnage and conflict, of earthquakes, pestilence, famine and woe, of purges and persecutions which dwarf all those of history. It tells of the crash of mighty empires, of anarchy, oppression and terror and wrath. It tells of an incarnate Beast, indwelt and driven by the Devil. It tells of war in heaven and war on earth. It goes from one horror to another. Its' martyrs are countless. Blood flows in crimson tides. Thunders roll, stars fall from heaven, seas turn to blood, seals are broken, trumpets are blown and vials of wrath are outpoured. Plagues surge up from the bottomless pit in the form of vast, countless armies mobilized by Satan himself. Men by the million march to Megeddo. Then the heavens split asunder, and there is a final invasion from outer space. It is Jesus, coming again! Backed by the armies of heaven.

But first, God speaks one word—"Peace!" For God would much rather make peace than He would wage war.

This is God's final peace offer. When He came the first time, the heralds from on high offered peace. When He appeared in the Upper Room, in resurrection power, He proclaimed peace. Now, before the end time wars and woes, He extends an olive branch one more time—"Peace!" He says, "Peace."

I was just a boy when World War 2 broke out in Britain. It broke out on a Sunday morning. In one of our churches, a man came in late. He had just heard the news. We were at war. He gave the news, and a solemn hush came over the people. War! A man got up and gave out a hymn. It went like this:

"Peace, perfect peace, in this dark world of sin?
the blood of Jesus whispers peace within.

"Peace, perfect peace, with sorrows surging 'round?
On Jesus' bosom nought but peace is found.

"Peace, perfect peace, with loved ones far away?
In Jesus' keeping we are safe, and they.

"Peace, perfect peace, the future all unknown?
Jesus we know and He is on the throne.

"Peace, perfect peace, death shadowing us and ours?
Jesus has conquered death and all its powers.

"IT IS ENOUGH! Earth's struggles soon shall cease
And Jesus call to heaven's perfect peace."

It is with some such thought in mind that Jesus begins this Apocalypse with an offer of lasting peace.

"Grace be unto you, and peace." Yes, indeed! For grace and peace with through at last. The storm clouds roll away. The drums of war are stilled, and the earth itself is purged with fire and there emerges a new heaven and a new earth where all is grace and peace.

AN OPENING BENEDICTION (3)
REVELATION 1:4-6

The Book of Revelation begins with a benediction. It speaks of all <u>the grace</u> that accrues to us, and of all <u>the glory</u> that accrues to Him. We begin with THE GRACE THAT ACCRUES TO US. In the first place, it is grace that <u>endures</u>: "Unto Him that loved us." Scholars tell us that the verb for love here is in the present tense. It should read "unto Him Who <u>loves</u> us. It is unconditional love as Moses, in his memoirs, made clear to Israel. "The Lord" he said, "did not set His love upon you because ye were more in number than any people: for yet were the fewest of all people, but because the Lord loved you" (Deut.7:7-8). Why does He love us? Because He loves us! It is unconditional love.

It is incomparable love. During one of his crusades in England, D. L. Moody was accosted by a young man named Henry Morehouse. "If I were to come to Chicago," he said, "would you let me preach in your church?" Moody gave a half promise, and then forgot about it. He did not expect that such a thing would happen.

Some while afterwards, who should turn up at Mr. Moody's door but young Henry Morehouse. "Hello, Mr. Moody," he said, "I have come to preach in your church." Trapped, D. L. Moody agreed to let him preach one night. "The fellow can't do much damage in one night," he confided to his deacons. "If he says anything out of line, I'll get up and correct him."

That night Henry Morehouse preached on John 3:16. He preached on the love of God. He preached with passion and power. D. L. Moody had never heard anything like it. It moved him deeply. It changed his whole concept of preaching. Indeed, Henry Morehouse became known as "the man who moved the man, who moved millions."

They asked him to preach again, and again, every night for a week. For a whole week Henry Morehouse preached on John 3:16 and on the love of God. At the end of the week, he said, "I have been trying to tell you how much God loves you. If I could borrow Jacob's ladder, if I could climb that shining stairway until I stood on the sapphire pavements of the city of God, if I could find Gabriel, the herald angel who stands in the presence of God and say to him, 'Gabriel, tell me, how much does God love the world?', I know what he would say. He would say to me, 'Henry Morehouse, God so loved the world He gave His only begotten Son that whosoever believeth in Him should never perish but have everlasting life."

Such is the grace that accrues to us. "Can anything separate us from the love of Christ?" says Paul. "Can trouble, pain or persecution? Can lack of clothes and food, danger to life and limb, the threat of force of arms? No! In all these things we are more than conquerors through Him that loved us. I am persuaded that neither death nor life, messenger from heaven or monarch of earth . . . nothing in God's whole world has any power to separate us from the love of God in Jesus Christ our Lord" (Rom.8:35-39).

"Unto Him Who <u>loves</u> us!" What a way to begin a book dedicated to an outpouring of God's wrath!

AN OPENING BENEDICTION (4)
REVELATION 1:4-6

In this beginning benediction, John sets before us THE GRACE THAT ACCRUES to us. It is grace that <u>endures</u>. The benediction is addressed to the One Who loves us and who keeps on loving us. It is also grace that <u>emancipates</u>: "Unto Him that has washed us from our sins . . . (some versions read "loosed us" from our sins). Dean Alford says there is a difference of only one letter between the two readings in the original. If we read: "Unto Him that <u>washed</u> us from our sins," then sin is regarded as a <u>stain</u>. If we read: "Unto Him that <u>loosed</u> us from our sins, then sin is regarded as a <u>chain</u>. Of course, it is BOTH.

<u>Sin is a stain</u>. When God wanted to teach this truth to His ancient people Israel He had them build the Tabernacle in the wilderness. At one end He sat in the Holy of Holies, a thrice-holy God, wrapped in the Shekinah glory. At the other end stood the sinner in all his guilt and need. The problem was how to bring that guilty sinner from "outside the camp" to "inside the veil." Even in his earliest, most tentative and initial steps, he was made aware that he was a man stained by sin.

He came first to the brazen altar. The great brazen alter, just inside the gate of the Tabernacle court was there to remind the sinner of his sin, to remind them he needed a <u>radical</u> cleansing from sin. Blood had to be shed.

Once he was past the brazen altar, he came to the brazen laver. He now discovered he needed a <u>recurrent</u> cleansing from sin. He had taken but a few steps; and, behold, he was defiled again. He needed to be washed in water, what Paul calls "the washing of water by the word" (Titus 3:5). sin is indeed a stain. The blood provides our radical cleansing, the Book provides our recurrent cleansing.

But sin is also a chain. Nobody, outside of the Bible, has caught that truth better than Charles Dickens in his famous book, <u>The Christmas</u>

Carol. He shows us old Ebenezer Scrooge sitting alone in his dingy room one Christmas Eve not suspecting he was about to receive a visit from the ghost of his dead partner, Jacob Marley. He was startled by the ringing of some disused bells in the far recesses of the house. "The bells ceased," says Dickens. "They were succeeded by a clanking noise deep down below, as if some person were dragging a heavy chain in the cellar."

Presently the ghost of Marley came in through the barred and bolted door. Scrooge recognized him at once. But the thing that riveted his attention was the chain that Marley clasped about his middle. It was long, and it wound about him like a tail. It was made of cash boxes, keys, padlocks, ledgers, deeds, and heavy purses wrought in steel.

"You are fettered," ventured Scrooge. "I wear the chain I forge in life," replied the ghost. "I made it of my own free will. Is its pattern strange to you? Or would you know the weight and length of the strong coil you wear yourself? It was full as heavy and as long as this seven Christmases ago. You have labored on it since. It is a ponderous chain."

And so it is. The strong chain of evil habit holds multitudes in its iron grip.

Well, thank God, Jesus has both <u>washed</u> us and <u>loosed</u> us. As the holy hymn says —

"He breaks the power of canceled sin,
And sets the <u>prisoner</u> free;
His blood can make the <u>foulest</u> clean,
His blood avails for me."

AN OPENING BENEDICTION (5)
REVELATION 1:4-6

This remarkable benediction celebrates THE GRACE THAT ACCRUES TO US. It is grace that endures. It is grace that emancipates. But it is also grace that <u>elevates</u>: "Unto Him that hath made us kings and priests unto God . . ."

Notice that word "made"—"He hath <u>made</u> us." It reminds us of the prodigal son. He had two prayers. He had a going-away prayer and he had a coming-home prayer. Here is his going-away prayer: "Father, <u>give</u> me!" It was a sinful, selfish prayer, the prayer of a young rebel tired of restraint, tired of goodness, longing for the far country with its fun, its freedom, its fraternities and its fast women and all. The Prodigal saw all these anticipated joys through starry eyes and he longed for them with eager desire. "Father, give me," he said. He needed cold cash to translate his dreams into deeds.

Here, by contrast, is his coming home-prayer: "Father, <u>make</u> me!" It was the prayer of a broken and a contrite heart. We see him, broken and bankrupt heading for home with faltering steps. He still had a long way to go when the father saw him and ran and had compassion, and fell on his neck and kissed him. "Make me as one of your hired servants." That was to be his prayer. But before ever he got to that part, the father broke in with a cry for a robe and a ring and for a fine, fatted calf for a feast. He was going to show this son of his how a father can love, and how a father can loose, and how a father lift.

Just so with God! His is grace that endures, grace that emancipates and grace that elevates: "Unto Him that hath <u>made</u> us," cries John. He has made us kings and priests unto God. That is to say, He has bestowed on us all the majesty of a prince, and all the ministry of a priest. This is His offer, in the Apocalypse, to a generation living on the edge of fearful judgment. It is His offer to us, and to our degenerate generation today.

The benediction closes by celebrating all THE GLORY THAT ACCRUES TO HIM. "To Him be glory and dominion for ever and ever." Note, first, it is <u>personal</u> glory—"To <u>Him</u> by glory."

When Queen Victoria celebrated her Diamond Jubilee, she had been on the throne of Britain for sixty years. She ruled the largest empire in history, an empire spread out over a quarter of the land mass of the world. A procession was arranged to celebrate her glory. Troops from a score of countries that owned her sway marched past her in triumph. The crowned heads of Europe came. Some forty Indian rajas marched. The world sent its delegates. But it was really <u>her</u> glory. As Mark Twain put it: "The Queen herself was the real procession. All the rest was embroidery." Just so with Jesus. "To <u>Him</u> be glory. It is His and His by right.

To <u>Him</u> be glory. It is personal glory. No one else can compare with Him. But it is also <u>positional</u> glory: "To Him be glory and dominion. The dominion Adam threw away in the garden of Eden has been retaken by

Christ. Now all glory and all dominion belongs to Him. It will be displayed to all the world one of these days.

Finally it is <u>perpetual</u> glory: "to Him be power and dominion for ever and ever." It will be displayed on earth for a thousand years during the Lord's Millennial reign. But men will tire of that in the end. Their unregenerate hearts will loath His iron rule of righteousness and long for the merry old days when sin could be indulged. Satan will find them easy dupes to his final batch of lies. Even that golden millennial age will pass away. It will be replaced by a new heaven and a new earth. Vast new empires in space will be created, and glory and dominion cheered and unchallenged, will fill all of God's endless domains "for ever and ever." Blessed be God! Well might we sing:

> *"To Him Whom men despise and slight*
> *To Him be glory given.*
> *The crown is His and His by right*
> *The highest place in heaven."*

A SCENE IN GLORY (1)

REVELATION 4-5

Most of what we know about heaven we know from the Book of Revelation. The scenes in the book alternate between heaven and earth. A scene on earth is followed by a scene in heaven. A scene in heaven is followed by a scene on earth. It is as though John, choking on the miasmas of a putrid planet, is constantly invited by God to come on up to heaven for a breath of fresh air.

The throne of God is mentioned seventeen times in these two short chapters. God wants John to know that, no matter what happens on earth, <u>He</u> is still on the throne. In chapter four the throne is a throne of <u>government</u>. In chapter five it is a throne of <u>grace</u>. In chapter four Jesus is worshipped as the <u>Lord of creation</u>. In chapter five He is worshipped as the <u>Lamb of Calvary</u>. In chapter four they sing: "Thou are worthy for Thou hast created . . ." He is worshipped as the <u>Author of creation</u>. In chapter five they sing: "Thou art worthy for Thou wast slain . . ." He is worshipped as the <u>Author of redemption</u>.

John comes away from this encounter with Heaven (and Heaven's view of earth's affairs) with a three-fold remembrance. He carries with him the memory of an unforgettable <u>throne</u>; the memory of an unforgettable <u>throng</u> and the memory of an unforgettable <u>thrill</u>, the thrill of seeing the Lord Jesus step into the spotlight of eternity, and become the center of everything.

We begin with THE UNFORGETTABLE THRONE. We note at once there is a <u>mystery</u> connected with that throne. For instance, look at the rainbow. Unlike earthly rainbows, with which we are so familiar, this heavenly rainbow is emerald in color and completely circular in form. And who are the mysterious "living creatures?" Who are they? And who are the four and twenty elders? Even more astonishing, God is described as a stone! We are accustomed to His being likened to various mundane things, to a shepherd, for instance, or to a human father, but to a <u>stone</u>? We are shrouded here in mystery. These mysterious things remind us that there are aspects of God's rule we shall never comprehend down here.

Just the same the fact that God is likened to a jasper and to a sardius stone should not surprise us. These were the first and last stones in the High Priest's breastplate. This echo from the Old Testament, and its reminder of the High Priest of Israel, and his ministry of intercession, draws our attention to the tender mercies and loving kindness of our God we learn that, no matter how severe the judgments which follow, God is too loving to be unkind, and too wise to make any mistakes. For the High Priest of old wore the breastplate, with the jasper and sardius stones, on his <u>heart</u>.

God, in mercy and loving kindness, has already lengthened out the day of grace for two thousand years. Now, beginning a book which deals primarily with judgment, judgment which can be postponed no longer, God still delays. He writes chapter after chapter, revealing Himself to us in this way and in that, putting off, for yet another paragraph or two, the dreadful business now in hand. How like God! He is God of might and miracle, of course; but, above all, He is a God of mercy most of all.

A SCENE IN GLORY (2)

REVELATION 4-5

There is a mystery connected with the throne, as it looms up before us in Revelation 4. There is a <u>majesty</u> connected with it, too. John details seven things about it. They give us glimpses of just what the judgment will be like that emanates from that throne of mystery and majesty.

First, it will be <u>flawless judgment</u>: the throne of God, as seen by John, was wrapped around with a rainbow. It described a perfect circle, a circle, of course, being recognized emblem of perfection. There will be no mistakes, no miscarriage of judgment, no grounds for appeal. It will be flawless judgment.

It is emerald in color, the color of earth, for the coming judgment has to do with the earth. Then, too, the fact that it is a <u>rainbow</u> which encircles the throne also points us back to earth. The rainbow, in the bible, is associated with the judgment of the Flood. God's judgment, then, when it bursts in all its fury on the earth, will be flawless and related to His covenant with the earth.

It will also be <u>formal judgment</u>. Twenty-four thrones surround the throne of God. The elders seated on these thrones are the crowned royalties of heaven, creatures of high rank in God's government of the universe. They form a celestial jury. Their role, however, is not to decide the question of guilt. That is all too evident. These watching elders have no need to weigh evidence. The handwriting of God is already etched on the consciences of all. Guilt is already established beyond all question the function of these elders is to declare their approval of God's decisions. The elders add another touch of formality and dignity to the court.

Then, too, it will be <u>fearful judgment</u>. Thunderings shake the precincts of the court. Dreadful lightning's strike terror into the hearts of those arraigned. As Moses on Sinai, surrounded by similar manifestations of God's holiness and power, did "exceedingly fear and quake," so those summoned here will be gripped by terror. They will tremble in mortal fear.

Moreover, it will be <u>factual judgment</u>. John saw the Holy Spirit there in all His plenitude. He is described in the plural under the title, "the seven

126

spirits of God," possibly a reference to His seven-fold attributes as described in Isaiah 11:2. He is now in Court as Prosecutor of all human race. He is there to convict people of sin, of righteousness and of judgment. He knows every thought, every word and every deed of every man, and every woman, and every child. He knows the time, the place, the occasion, the motive and the consequences. In this life, God offers people a fair trial, or a free pardon. If it is a fair trial they choose, that is what they will get. It will send them to a lost eternity.

Then, too it will be fundamental judgment. The Cherubim are there. In Genesis 3 they are associated with God's creatorial rights and they come to guard the gate of Eden. In Exodus they are associated with God's redemptive rights, they overshadow the mercy seat with their wings. They are the executives of His government and His grace. Here now in heaven, actively responding to God's acts of judgment, they watch to ensure that all His rights are upheld and owned.

Moreover, it will be final judgment. John saw a sea of glass. The sea is the very symbol of restless change. A sea of glass suggests that everything is now permanent and beyond all change. It is too late for the kind of repentance which won reprieve for in the days of Jonah. Men have sinned away the day of grace. Nothing can now be changed. There is no court of appeal. This is the ultimate supreme court of the universe. What men have sown they now must reap.

Finally, it will be fatal judgment. The terrifying thing in all this is that there is no lamb in chapter 4, no lamb at all. It was this very thing which haunted Isaac on his way to Mount Moriah. He saw the knife, which spoke of death; and he saw the fire, which spoke of that which comes after death. But where was the lamb? (Gen.22) To be brought before this throne, and this court, without the Lamb will be fatal indeed.

Such, then, is the majesty of the throne before which all those who have no Lamb will one day appear. How we can thank God for the Lamb of God which takes away the guild and stain of all our sin (Jno.1:29).

A SCENE IN GLORY (3)

REVELATION 4-5

So, then, John comes away from the Glory Land with the memory of an unforgettable THRONE. He comes away, moreover, with the memory of an unforgettable THRONG.

The cherubim are there. The elders are there, countless angels are there, the redeemed are there. He draws our attention to the cherubim. They acknowledge the One upon the throne as the holiest One in the universe.

John draws our attention to the singleness of their function: "They cease not day and night saying, Holy! Holy! Holy! Lord God Almighty, which was and is and is to come." They acknowledge Him as Jehovah, the One Who transcends time.

The cherubim appear to be the highest of all created beings. Lucifer was "the anointed cherub," before he fell, a high-ranked member of their order. The cherubim John saw summon up the vast resources of their giant intellects, the fathomless depths of their emotions, and the ceaseless drive and force of their volitional powers; and they worship. Worship is the one, great, supreme, overriding activity of heaven. These sinless sons of light see the acts of God, Most High. They weigh His words and ways, and their instinctive response is to worship. "Holy! Holy! Holy!" they cry. "He was! He is! He is to come!" "Holy! Holy! Holy!" Elsewhere we learn that God is love. Here we learn that God is holy. Thoughts of God's love melt the heart of His friends in tenderness. Thoughts of God's holiness melt the hearts of His foes in terror.

So, then, we note the singleness of their function as they stand before His throne. John then draws our attention to the singularity of their form. One looked like a lion, one like a calf, one looked like a man and one looked like a flying eagle.

The first had the face of a lion. When Matthew took it in hand to give us a picture of Christ, that is exactly what he portrayed, a lion. The Lord Jesus was the Lion of the Tribe of Judah, royal and rightful heir to David's throne.

Mark, by contrast, portrayed an ox. On one side of that ox was a plow, on the other side an altar. Like a banner over all was the proclamation,

128

"Ready for either." Mark shows Him as the One willing to give His life in service and willing to give His life in sacrifice.

<u>Luke</u> had yet another portrait. He shows us a Man, One perfect in His humanity, peerless in His holiness and prodigal in His helpfulness.

<u>John</u>, by contrast, draws the picture of a flying eagle. He shows us the One Who came down from above, Who's true home was up yonder, beyond the blue, in highest heaven.

Such was Jesus. He was like a lion, like an ox, like a man and like an eagle. Such, too, were the cherubim. As they gazed upon the Lord in glory, each one takes on somewhat of His likeness. <u>One</u> was like a lion, <u>one</u> was like an ox, <u>one</u> was like a man and <u>one</u> was like a man and <u>one</u> was like an eagle. Not even a cherub could take on <u>all</u> His likeness, but each one reflected something of it just the same.

The more time we spend with Jesus, the more we get to look like Him. Moses, for instance, came down from the mount with his face aglow. Stephen's face shone like an angel's. A glance will save. As the old hymn says, "There is life for a <u>look</u> at the crucified One" (John 3:14-15; Numb. 21:9); it is the gaze, however, that sanctifies. "We all," says Paul, "beholding as in a glass the glory of the Lord are changed into the same image from glory to glory, even as by the Spirit of the Lord" (2 Cor.3:18).

LET THERE BE LIGHT
GENESIS 1:3-4

"Light be!" God said. "Light was," the Holy Spirit says. Just like that! Light is a mysterious thing. It travels at an astonishing 186,000 miles per second. In one second it can travel around the earth seven and a half times. Its speed is always constant. It never changes. The speed of light is at the heart of the famous equation which ushered in the Nuclear Age—E-MC2 (energy equals mass multiplied by the speed of light squared). Light be! Light was!

It is not enough, however, to grasp the obvious, surface meaning of these words, that God brought light into being and chased away the darkness. God's Word is <u>God's</u> Word, so naturally it has depths upon depths to be explored. It is as fathomless as the being of God is Himself. The Bible was not written to be a handbook of science, though whenever it has occasion to speak on a subject which falls within the domain of science it does so with infallible, inerrant accuracy. The Bible is a handbook of salvation. Things which we can find out by a process of human <u>reasoning</u> are left to us to discover for ourselves, the physics of light, for instance. Things we cannot know by mere reasoning are made known to us by a process of Divine <u>revelation</u>. As truth is revealed by God in His Word, so light is shed abroad in our hearts and our understanding is opened to truth about which, before, we were in darkness.

Paul shows us how to look for deeper, spiritual truth beneath the surface of, for instance, a narrative portion of Scripture. He takes his illustration from our text here in Genesis 1:3-4. God said, "Light be," and light was. That is the obvious, outward, surface statement which barely needs comment. Paul ignores the physical aspect, the creation of light in the universe, and concentrates on the deeper, spiritual aspect. He says: "God, Who commanded the light to shine out of darkness hath shined in our hearts to give the light of the knowledge of the glory of God in the face of Jesus Christ (2 Cor. 4:6). Beyond the creation story, Paul saw the redemption story. Doubtless there are even deeper depths to be discovered in the statement, "Light be, and light was." It will take us all eternity to explore all the unsuspected depths beneath the surface of God's Word.

It is John however, who expounds the typology of light. He begins with <u>the light shining</u>. Jesus, he says, is "the true light" (John 1:9). He well remembered Jesus' own words: "I am the light of the world" (John 8:12), and the sneering response of His foes. He is "the true light that lighteth every man that cometh into the world." God sees to it that all people receive some measure of light. Jesus is the Light of the world.

Satan is the prince of darkness and wields enormous power. But he cannot stop the Light from shining. He tried it at Calvary, and failed. The darkness, John says, could not "comprehend" (<u>katalambano</u>) "overcome" the Light (John 1:5). It never can. The world did what it could to overcome and overpower He Who was the Light of the world" at Calvary. It failed. He, the Light of the world, was so completely in charge of things, that even while He hung upon the tree, actually put out the sun and plunged the land in darkness for three intermmable terrifying hours. Just before He died He turned it on again (Matt.27:45). The world thought it had put out the Light, once and for all, when they sealed Him in His tomb. Not a bit of it! He came marching back in triumph holding aloft the very keys of death. Satan tries to put out the light of the Gospel everywhere it shines. He cannot win (Matt.16:18). Already the light shines around the world and, in a day soon to come, it will dazzle every eye.

John tells us also of the light showing. Light exposes the hidden works of darkness. And "this is the condemnation, that light is come into the world, and men loved darkness rather than light" (3:19). No where was this more evident than when the members of the Sanhedrin, instead of responding to the amazing news that Christ was alive from the dead with joy and awe, tried desperately instead to stifle it with lying propaganda and organized persecution of the Church. "They will not come to the Light," John said, "lest their deeds should be exposed" (3:20). For them, and their like, Jude says, "is reserved the blackness of darkness for ever" (V.13).

"Light be," God says. "Light was," the Holy Spirit says. All those who open up their hearts to this light will find that "the path of the just is as a shining light that shineth more and more unto the perfect day" (Prov.4:18).

THE LESSER LIGHT
GENESIS 1:16

The moon is about one quarter of the size of earth. It orbits the earth at a mean distance of 238,866 miles and at an average speed of 2,287 miles an hour. It takes it a little over twenty-seven days to complete one orbit. Its temperature soars to 215°F in the sun and sinks to -250°F in the shade. The moon has fascinated mankind from the early dawn of time. People in their ignorance have worshipped it. Abraham, before he met the true and living God, dwelt at Ur, a center of moon worship in his day. Possibly he once worshipped it himself.

The moon was doubtless created "in the beginning" when God created the heaven and the earth. According to the Genesis creation narrative, the moon was appointed to function on the fourth day of creation. It is from the movement of the sun we get our concept of the year and the day; it is from the movement of the moon we get our concept of the month.

The moon is of interest to us theologically. It can be viewed, for instance, as a type of the Church. Consider, first, the origin of the moon, a matter which has been the subject of considerable debate. One view is that it was spun off from the surface of the earth and that the vast cavity, now filled by the Pacific Ocean, was one result of this. If that is so, then the moon was once part of this world but is now seated on high in the heavens and, as such, gives us a picture of believers who comprise the Church. The Church is made up of people who once belonged to Earth, but who are now seated with Christ in heavenly places, far above the restless world that wars below.

The function of the moon is to rule the night. It is seated on high to cast light upon the earth during the period when the sun is absent. It has no light of its own. The only way the moon can shine is by reflecting the light of the sun; but even at that, it can reflect only seven percent of the light that strikes its surface. In astronomical terms, the magnitude (i.e. the scale of brightness) of the full moon is very small. By contrast, the brightness of the sun's light is 400,000 times as great as that of the moon.

Similarly, the function of the Church is to shed light upon the earth during the dark period covered by the absence of Christ. The light the Church spreads is very dim, however, as compared with the light of Christ. But, pale as it is by comparison, with the light of Christ, the light believers bring to bear on human affairs is better than nothing at all. The Church does not generate light; for, like the moon, it has no light of its own. It reflects the light of Christ. That, in itself is a most important role.

The moon waxes and wanes, all the way from a full, bright disk down to a small crescent and even into darkness itself. Moreover, it can be eclipsed. This happens when the earth comes between the moon and the sun. In like manner, there are times in the history of the Church revival comes and when the church shines very brightly indeed. The world benefits greatly from its light at such times. There are other times, however, when the testimony of the Church grows dim; and darkness reigns. Tragically, too, there are times of apostasy when the Church succumbs to the philosophies and errors of the world; and its light is eclipsed.

Then, too, the moon exercises power over the tides. Twice every day it pulls the waters of the oceans up along the shorelands and into the rivers of the earth. The seas are powerless, great as they are, to resist the tremendous influence of the moon, though it seems so remote and far away. In the typology of Scripture, the <u>seas</u> represent the troubled, storm-tossed nations of the world, just as the <u>earth</u> represents the nation of Israel. The moon reminds us of the enormous influence the Church has had throughout history over the tides in the affairs of men. People discount the influence of the Church but that does not change the fact. The prayers of God's people and the preaching of its ambassadors, in the power of the Spirit, has its effect on every shore.

SEPARATING THE WATERS
GENESIS 1

The works of God in creation, as recorded in Genesis 1, illustrate the works of God in redemption. "Light be!" God said, and light was. It is a lesson in SALVATION. God begins by shedding light into a sin-darkened soul. Darkness is dispelled. People see the truth. Their eyes are opened to see beauty in Christ. The power of darkness, including the power of spiritual darkness, is real enough; but it cannot triumph over light for ever.

God's next movement in creation was to bring order out of chaos. He separated the waters from the waters. It is a lesson in SANCTIFICATION. There came into being two vast seas, "the waters below" and "the waters above; the sea, and that vast ocean suspended in space in the form of clouds. There are some 54 trillion, 460 billion tons of it, defying gravity and riding the hidden highways of the sky.

The waters below are virtually identical with the waters above. Both are made up of two parts of hydrogen and one part of oxygen. They are kept separate by means of an atmosphere. And their behavior is different.

The waters below always seek their lowest level. Their nature is to go down. Rivers have their origins high in the mountains, but they end up in the depths of the sea. The Amazon, for instance, has its source in the high wind-swept Andes of Peru closer to the Pacific than the Atlantic towards which it flows. Down it goes, thundering ever downward and gathering into its embrace other downward-flowing streams as it goes. By the time it reaches the ocean, it is a vast inland sea, with banks sixty miles apart, draining half a continent. Such, too, is the nature of man, born in sin. No man can lift himself back to the state of innocence which marked Adam and Eve before the Fall. The second law of thermodynamics, which explains how everything is running down, from order to chaos, has to counterpart in the spiritual realm—in "the law of sin and death!"

The waters above, by contrast, represent those who have been redeemed. Clouds are comprised of water which has been brought under the influence and power of the sun. This water has been <u>changed</u> by evaporation. It rises to the heavens above and rides the currents of the air. These two oceans are separated by an atmosphere, what the Bible calls the firmament. In the form of a stream, transformed water can be <u>channeled</u> and put to work in the world.

It is essentially "atmosphere" which distinguishes between unregenerate people and those who have been redeemed by Christ "the sun of righteousness" (Mal.4:2) and raised on high to sit with Him in heavenly places. The redeemed enjoy the atmosphere of the prayer meeting, the Bible class, the worship service. The lost seek the atmosphere of the ballroom, the tavern, and the theater. The atmosphere of the one is alien and foreign and unpleasant to the other.

Finally, God separated the sea from the land. The land was raised up from prairie to mountain peak. It is a lesson in SOVEREIGNTY. In the symbolism of Scripture, the sea represents the nations of mankind, restless, storm-tossed and troubled. The land symbolizes the nation of Israel, set in the midst of the nations and, constantly attacked by its rulers but never subdued.

So creation points us to redemption and shows us God at work in salvation, sanctification and sovereignty.

THE TEMPTATION OF EVE
GENESIS 3:1

He is called "the old serpent." Three chapters in from the beginning of the Bible we see him for the first time; three chapters in from the end of the Bible we see him for the last time. He came into the garden of Eden to effect the fall and ruin of the human race. He will end up in the eternal flames of the lake of fire.

His first goal in the garden was to disarm Eve by robbing her of the only weapon she had, the Word of God. The Bible Eve had was small enough—just two brief verses, but it was enough. Sadly, she misquoted it three times. Twice she subtracted from what God had actually said, and once she added to it. After that she was in Satan's power. Satan based his attack on a <u>doubt</u>, a <u>denial</u> and a <u>delusion</u>, and swiftly carried the day.

"Yea hath God said?" That was the <u>doubt</u>. How do you know God said that? You only have it by transmission from Adam. You weren't there when this "Word" was given. How can you prove it is the Word of God? How do you know it is true?

"Thou shalt <u>not</u> surely die!" That was the <u>denial</u>. How ridiculous! Death for eating fruit from a tree! What nonsense! Besides, God is a loving God. Can you seriously believe that God would put you to death just for taking a bite from a piece of fruit? Death? There is nothing to fear about death. Death is the greatest adventure of all. God just wants to frighten you. In any case, you won't die. You'll begin to live.

"Ye shall be as gods." That was the <u>delusion</u>. It was the promise of freedom from narrowness and from unacceptable restrictions on one's behavior. It promised access to a wonderful, glorious world of knowledge. Life in a new dimension could be hers. She could become a liberated woman.

Inherent in the temptation was an appeal to "the lust of the eyes" because the tree was "pleasant to the eyes." There was an appeal to "the lust of the flesh" because the tree was good for food. There was an appeal to "the pride of life" because it was "to be desired to make one wise." This threefold appeal promised access to mysterious and marvelous hidden secrets. They themselves Adam and Eve would become like God Himself.

The serpent's wiles were successful. In fact, he has not had to change his approach throughout all the course of human history. For all temptation rises from these three primeval appeals.

Once Eve had accepted the Devil's lie and rejected God's truth the rest followed as a matter of course. Satan led Eve from one foolish act to another, each downward step preparing the way for the next one.

First, "she saw." The serpent fastened her gaze upon the desired object. Soon she could not take her eyes off it. A large percentage of temptation comes to us through our eyes. The plan was to turn the look into a lust.

Next, "she took." Now the plan was to turn the desire into a deed. That had to be her decision. Satan can persuade but he cannot push. He could suggest to the Lord, for instance, that He throw Himself down from the temple pinnacle; but he could not push Him down.

Then, "she did eat." Now the plan was to turn the choice into a chain. Jesus said, "He that committeth sin is the slave of sin" (John 8:34). Habits grow. They are flimsy enough at first, but each time we repeat the deed, the power of the habit is increased, until the habit itself takes over the will and we find ourselves in chains.

Finally, "she gave." That was the ultimate goal. The sinner became a seducer. It is significant that the serpent did not tempt Adam, Eve did.

Thus "sin entered" and death by sin. The fall was complete. Satan had won. Death reigned. Satan had won? Not forever! For Jesus came, and the serpent was no match for Him. His little bag of tricks was scorned by Christ. Satan lost, and now he lives in terror of the return from heaven of the victorious Christ. And well he might.

BOLDNESS TO ENTER

HEBREWS 10:19-20

For some 1500 years the veil had hung between the Holy Place and the Holy of Holies in tabernacle and temple in Jerusalem. It served one purpose—to keep people out of the presence of God. It was death to go beyond that veil. Indeed, it was death, for anyone not born into the family of Aaron to go anywhere near the veil. Calvary changed all that. The veil was rent when Jesus died and believers are now invited to come boldly right in to the presence of God.

Let us get the full impact of that. Picture an Old Testament Moabite finding his way to the gate of the tabernacle and there being stopped by the keeper of the gate. The conversation might go something like this:

Keeper: "Who are you?"

Moabite: "I'm a man from Moab. I have heard about your God. I should like to go in there and worship Him."

Keeper: "You can't do that. The Law of our God bans a Moabite from the worship of God until his tenth generation."

Moabite: "What would I have to do to escape this curse of the Law of your God?"

Keeper: "You would have to born again. You would have to be born an Israelite, be born of one of the tribes of Dan, shall we say, or Ephraim or Judah."

Moabite: "I wish I'd been born an Israelite, of the tribe of Judah. I would go in and help those people who are serving the altar. I could help them carry away the ashes, perhaps, or help them move the tabernacle when you people march on from place to place."

Keeper: "Oh, no! You couldn't do that. You would need to be born a Levite, for only people of the tribe of Levi can touch those things."

Moabite: "I wish I had been born an Israelite, of the tribe of Levi. What I should really like to do is help those robed priests with their work with sacrifices at the altar there. I could help lift those heavy animals onto the altar, perhaps."

Keeper: "No, you could not do that. You would have to be born not only of the tribe of Levi but also of the family of Aaron. Only Aaron's sons can be priests."

Moabite: "I wish I had been born an Israelite, of the tribe of Levi, a priest of the family of Aaron. I should like to go in there, into that covered shrine yonder. I see priests going in and out of there at times. Tell me, what is it like in there?"

Keeper: "It is very beautiful in there, all gleaming gold, rich color and costly linen. There is a golden table in there, a golden lampstand and a golden altar. Then there is a veil, thick, costly, and beautiful. Beyond that veil is what we call "the Holy of Holies." It contains the ark of the covenant, with its mercy seat. You can see that cloudy pillar which overshadows the camp of Israel. You see how it rests upon the tabernacle? God dwells in that cloud. It not only overshadows God's people, it actually sits upon the mercy seat upon the ark."

Moabite: "Oh, that I had been born a priest of the family of Aaron. I would love to go beyond the veil and worship your God in that holy, holy place."

Keeper: "Oh, no. You couldn't do that. Only the High Priest can go in there. You would need to be born of the house of Eleazar of the family of Aaron, of the tribe of Levi and of the nation of Israel before ever you could even think of going in there. God's High Priests come from the house of Eleazer."

Moabite: "I wish I had been born an Israelite, of the tribe of Levi, of the family of Aaron and of the house of Eleazer. I would go in there again and again. I would go in three times a day. I would stay long hours in there worshipping your God."

Keeper: "Oh no! Even the High Priest can only go in there once a year, on the day of atonement, and, even then, only after taking the most elaborate ritual precautions. Moreover, he cannot tarry in there. He must present the blood of the sacrifice before the mercy seat and then hurry out again. So you see Mr. Moabite, you have no hope whatsoever of entering "inside the veil."

Sadly we see the Moabite turn away.

But that was before Calvary. When Jesus died, God tore the veil in two (Matt.27:51). Now He invites all believers to come in. We are to have boldness to "enter into the holiest by the blood of Jesus." We can come as often as we like, we can stay as long as we like, we can talk to Him about whatever we like. It is a miracle of grace. God has given us this priceless privilege. It should fill our hearts with wonder, love and praise. It should move us to spend much time in there, where Jesus sits enthroned.

FAITH DENIED

HEBREWS 11:1

"Faith," says the Holy Spirit, "is the substance of things hoped for, the evidence of things unseen." The word for "substance" here is <u>hupostasis</u>. Paul uses the word to describe the person of the Lord Jesus as expressing the very image of God in human form (1:3). In everyday Greek the word was used to depict title deeds. A title deed gives substance to a person's claim to property. The word for "evidence" is <u>elenchos</u>. It means "proof."

Two thoughts emerge. Faith gives us the title deeds to things hoped for, and it gives us all the evidence we need that certain things we have not yet seen are all they are said to be. In other words, faith has to do with things we <u>long for</u>, things still unsatisfied as yet; and it has to do with things we <u>look for</u>, things still unseen as yet. In both cases faith makes them substantial and real. Faith is not wishful thinking. "Faith comes by hearing and hearing by the Word of God" (Rom.10:17).

<u>Abraham</u> shows us how faith is the title deed, the guarantee, the substance of things hoped for. Abraham longed for a son. The years passed, and the son did not come. He grew older. He passed the age when he could still hope.

Paul tells us that Abraham "against hope believed in hope. . . . and being not weak in faith, he considered not his own body now dead, when he was about a hundred years old, neither yet the deadness of Sarah's womb: he staggered not at the promise of God through unbelief; but was strong in faith, giving glory to God. And being full persuaded that, what He had promised, He was able also to perform" (Rom.4:18-21).

Abraham's faith in God was so strong that the thing he longed for was a real possession of his before ever the promised son was born. That is to say, he already had the boy's birth certificate in his hand (in God's pledged Word), before he had the child in his arms. God's Word was the ground of his faith and assurance. The thing he longed for was already his—by faith.

<u>Noah</u> shows us how faith is "the evidence, the proof of things unseen." God told Noah He was going to send a flood. It seems likely that Noah had never seen a flood. Genesis 2:6 would indicate he had never even seen rain,

never seen the window of heaven opened, never seen the fountains of the great deep erupt. Certainly he had never seen God act in universal, catastrophic judgment.

But God had spoke, and Noah believed God and set out to obey Him by building the ark even though there were no actual signs of the promised Flood. In sure anticipation of things not seen as yet, but most surely to be expected in God's time, Noah build the ark. The threatened judgment was delayed for 120 years. The ark was finished at last and still sure that the Flood would come, Noah and his family entered the ark and still the flood did not come. Nothing happened for a whole week, but Noah had no doubt. God's Word was God's Word. A week later, and the proof based on faith became proof based on fact. The rain began to fall.

The principle of faith, whether relating to things <u>longed</u> for or things <u>looked</u> for applies to us as well. God's Word is <u>sure</u>.

By Faith We Understand (1)
Hebrews 11:3

Hebrews 11 is the picture gallery of faith. A host of Old Testament giants are portrayed in that chapter. We meet Abel and Enoch, Noah and Abraham, Isaac and Jacob, all people whose faith turned them into giants. But the list begins with <u>US</u>! "By faith WE . . ." the sacred writer says. "By faith <u>we</u> understand that the worlds were framed by the Word of God." There is an alternate reading (By faith we understand that the ages were formed by the Word of God), but, for now, we shall let the statement stand as it is.

We gaze about us at globes and galaxies, and we stand in awe at the Word of God which spoke them into being. The meaning of the text as found in the Authorized Version is obvious enough. God's Word brought into existence the great empires of space.

Let us take our own star, the sun, as an example. It is 93 million miles away from us (a distance equivalent to more than 18,000 round trips between San Francisco and New York). According to astronomers, it is five billion years old. It is 667 times larger than the earth. The temperature of the sun's interior is about 29 million degrees Fahrenheit. It has a diameter of 864,000 miles, and it weighs a billion billion billion tons.

It is the center of a solar system. That solar system consists of the sun, nine planets, 32 moons and some 100,000 asteroids and 100 billion comets. The earth's immediate neighbors in space are Mercury, Venus and Mars. The remotest planet is Pluto, an oddball planet with a peculiar orbital path around the sun, quite different from that of other planets. So great is the sun's gravitational sway, its influence extends to a distance a thousand times farther than the orbit of Pluto before its power begins to be canceled by the pull of other stars.

All this was framed by the Word of God. But our sun, solar system and sphere are only a puny part of the story. Our sun is one star, and a moderate star at that, in a galaxy of 100 billion stars. We call that galaxy the Milky Way. It has a diameter of 100,000 light years—an inconceivable 600 million billion miles. The sun is located 30,000 light years from the hub of the galaxy which it orbits once every 200 million years.

But there are 100 billion other galaxies in known space besides our own. Some of them are receding from us at speeds close to the speed of light (186,000 miles per second). All this was framed by the Word of God.

Outer space is full of wonders. The Great Orion Nebula, for instance, is a vast cradle for the birth of new stars. It has enough raw material for 10,000 stars the size of our sun. More than fifty percent of all stars are binaries, two stars moving through space together. Sometimes a star known as a supernova explodes. When that occurs, a compressed core remains. We call it a neutron star. A pinhead's worth of neutron star material weights about a million tons!

And so it goes, on and one, a vast, fascinating universe of worlds made by the Word of God. The Word of God says so. And God cannot lie. What words! What worlds!

BY FAITH WE UNDERSTAND (2)

HEBREWS 11:3

"By faith we understand that the worlds were framed by the Word of God." According to the surface meaning, this statement draws our attention to the great empire of space. Beyond our own small globe, beyond a hundred billion galaxies, before the beginning of time, is God in all His omnipotent power, putting forth His Word and bringing it all into being. Faith accepts that to be so.

Some, however, see a different picture here. The word for "worlds" is aion, meaning "an age." If rendered that way then, of course, the verse tells us that the ages, the various epochs of time, were framed by the Word of God. In this case, our understanding is directed not to God's activity in creation but to His activity in redemption. Faith soars, not only at the omnipotence of God in making the heavens but also at the omniscience of God in making history. We see God pursuing His grand purposes in the redemption of Adam's ruined race being carried forward age after age. Page after page the Word of God reveals this governing activity of God in the onward march of human affairs. A correct understanding of God's plans and purposes, in dealing thus with the human race in different ways at difficult times, is essential to a proper understanding of the Word of God itself.

First, there was the age of innocence when Adam and Eve lived in the garden of Eden under ideal conditions. That age ended with the Fall and with the banishment of Adam and Eve from Paradise.

Next came the age of conscience. A knowledge of right and wrong was the one legacy the human race inherited from the Fall. This age also ended in judgment. Men became so wicked that God purged the earth with the Flood.

Then came the age of government. The sword of the magistrate was given to Noah, and the death penalty was instituted as a deterrent to high crime. But a descendent of Ham named Nimrod coveted the sword of the magistrate into the sword of the conqueror, turned it against his fellow men and tried to found a global society. The building of the tower of Babel was the final expression of all this godless humanism, materialism and rebellion against God's Word. Judgment followed.

The age of promise came next. God began again, this time with an individual, with Abraham to whom He gave many great and precious promises including possession of the Land of Canaan and of all the territory between the Nile and the Euphrates. The Promised Land seemed a remote possession, however, when the heirs of the promises found themselves in Egyptian bondage and facing total annihilation. Then Moses came to be their kinsman-redeemer and this nation of several million slaves was set free and headed for home—for the Promised Land. The speed with which the emancipated Hebrews, on their way from Egypt to Canaan, turned from God to idols, is eloquent. In Egypt they had learned that a sacred cow was one of Egypt's many gods. The swift acceptance by the Hebrews of Aaron's golden calf shows clearly that they were attracted to Egyptian idolatry. Their various apostasies in the wilderness on the way to Canaan exposed them to judgment and great peril.

Next came the age of law. Moses, having emancipated the enslaved Hebrews, gave them God's law, and brought the people to the borders of the Promised Land. The Mosaic Law, given at Sinai, was summed up in ten basic commandments (Exodus 20). It was expanded in the Pentateuch to 613 commandments covering all aspects of life. This age lasted through the days of the Theocracy, the Monarchy and the Dependency. It ended when God set Israel aside for the rejection of Christ and put an end to Judaism as a religion He could bless.

Then followed the age of grace (the Church Age). During this long period God has been calling out a people and baptizing them into the Church, the mystical body of Christ.

This age will be followed by the age of wrath. God will rapture His Church and then pour out His wrath upon Israel and the nations.

Then will come the millennial age during which Christ will reign on earth in power and glory.

Finally, the ages to come will be inaugurated by the creation of a new heaven and a new earth.

Thus, sovereignly, God tests a man under various conditions. It was not that God had any need to experiment in hope of finding a system that would work. The purpose of all these changes in God's handling of human affairs was to prove to fallen man how utterly sinful and fallen he is and how completely dependent on God he is for salvation and he is everlasting life.

BY FAITH ENOCH WAS TRANSLATED
GENESIS 5:21-24; HEBREWS 11

"There were giants in the earth in those days," God says. They appeared in the godless line of Cain. They were prodigies of strength, knowledge and wickedness. But there were other giants, too, unheralded and unsung, mighty men of God, giants of the faith. There were men like Seth, the founder of the godly line, men like Noah and Enoch who spoke to contemporary issues, warning of judgment to come, and Abel, noble martyr of the faith. Our thoughts here are taken up with Enoch. The first man to leave this earth was Abel. He died, both murdered and martyred, hero and saint. The second man was Enoch—caught up boldly into heaven by way of the rapture. A giant indeed!

We think first of HIS TIMES. They overlapped with "the days of Noah and displayed the same hallmark. It was a time of great mental activity. Cain, a vagabond of a man, surprisingly enough, conceived the idea of gathering an ever-growing world population into cities. Rural lifestyles, with their innate conservation gave way to urban living. Great cities attract talent and breed crime. It was so in Enoch's day. All fields of human endeavor experienced tremendous innovations and growth. Science, engineering and technology took gigantic strides and produced the skills needed to build the ark. Art expressed itself in music entertainment food processing came into its own and marketing. It was God Who enabled them to achieve these things and to fill their houses with good things. Their response was to tell God to be gone. What could the Almighty do for them they could not do for themselves (Job.22:16-18).

So it was not only a time of mental activity it was also a time of material prosperity. They were eating and drinking and marrying and giving in marriage, all legitimate things but things which were blighted by their unbelief.

144

Moreover it was a time of <u>moral depravity</u>. "The earth was corrupt", the Holy Spirit declared. Men employed their imaginative powers to devise wicked pleasures and pastimes. Their every thought was evil. They lived to gratify their lusts and to pursue pornography and perversion with the blessing of all.

Finally it was an age of <u>monumental apostasy</u>. The godly line dwindled to the sum of one man's family. The Cainites abandoned all pretense of religion. Of the dozen names in the line of Cain, listed in the record, only two had any reference to God (Mehujael and Methusael). In contrast, those recorded in the godly line often have annotations alongside their names, comments which help us see how godliness was kept alive on the earth despite the increasing wickedness of the Cainites and the dwindling numbers of the Sethites.

The godlessness of the Cainites brought in the final apostasy. Occultism flourished and gave rise to a "New Age" movement. Men began to explore the deep things of Satan and to delve into forbidden secrets. Satan gave them fruit from a fatal tree of knowledge and their eyes were opened. They became as gods and plunged into the ultimate evil. A strange hybrid progeny appeared and wickedness inundated the earth.

We think next of HIS TESTIMONY. Enoch was the heir of the ages, descendant of a long line of patriarchs of the faith. The torch of testimony was handed on to him by his forebears, and he raised it high for 300 years before handing it on to his son. As apostasy increased, so Enoch preached the more boldly. He warned of the coming of the Lord in judgment. He foresaw a coming holocaust of wrath. He denounced ungodliness. He set a date for the day of doom. He called his son by the significant name "Methuselah"—"When he dies, it shall come." Not even such anointed preaching as Enoch's, however, could stem the tide. Wickedness was in the saddle, riding high, wide and handsome across the face of the world. Nothing could stop it but judgment.

Finally we have HIS TRANSLATION. For Enoch did not die. He was carried bodily into heaven. The rapture came; and he was gone, caught away in a moment, in the twinkling of an eye, from family and friends, from business partners and fellow saints. A voice for God was suddenly stilled on the earth. The ungodly took it in their stride, doubtless glad that he was gone. It would save them the trouble of killing him. A silence fell, an ominous silence, not broken until the voice of Noah rang out; and the judgment, long promised, finally fell. Thus Enoch was a candidate for rapture. So are we who love the Lord.

BY FAITH NOAH

HEBREWS 11

At last! The work was done. The great carpenter of the Old Testament had finished the work God had given him to do. A judgment-proof means of salvation had been provided for all. And at unknown but enormous cost. Giant trees had been felled, vast timbers had been hewn and hauled and hammered into place. All had proceeded according to plan. A blueprint for man's salvation, thought out in heaven, had been wrought out on earth.

The work had been vast. Blood and sweat and tears and toil had been the toll. But now the roof was on. Stalls and rooms and storage bins were all in place. All had been done according to plan.

Now came THE LAST ACTIVITY. The ark had to be made leakproof, safe and secure against sea and storm, howling wind and heaving wave. So pitch was prepared and applied, inside and out, over every inch of the surface of the ark, into every nook and cranny.

In terms of the type, it is significant that the Hebrew word for "pitch" is the same word used for "atonement." It means "to cover." The pitch kept the judgment waters of the flood out of the ark. Similarly atonement keeps the judgment out of the soul.

The pitch was lavishly applied. Then cautious Noah, pitch pot in one hand, brush in the other, inspected the ark one more time. It was done. It had been an enormous work. The ark, when finished, was the exact shape of a coffin. It would take those who trusted God through death to a new life in a new world.

Then came THE LAST APPEAL. Methuselah died. His longevity had become a legend even in an age when people lived a long, long time. His father, Enoch, had been a patriarch, a preacher and a prophet. He foretold the second coming of Christ and, nearer to his own age, the impending judgment of the Flood. He even set a date for it. "When he dies it shall come" was the prophetic name he gave to his son. And now Methuselah was dead. Probably Noah, a preacher of righteousness, preached Methuselah's funeral. "He is dead!" We can almost hear him cry, "It will come! The heavens will tear asunder. The storm is about to burst. Flee from the wrath to come. Salvation can be yours in the ark." But he preached in vain, his last sermon no more productive than his first one. He had preached for a hundred and twenty years, all the time the ark was being built. In vain! People thought he was a fool.

Then came THE LAST ANIMAL; in twos and in sevens the animals came. Big and small, wild and tame, an endless line of them. Until, at last, the final creature found its place on board. This parade of beasts and birds must have been an astonishing testimony to the godless people of earth. Still, they shrugged it off as some kind of a conjurer's trick. "Very clever! Great circus act! Wonder how he did it!" they would say.

Finally came THE LAST ACT. Noah and his family, just eight people, went on board the ark. A last look around! A final call to some wavering person! A last glimpse of the cloudless sky! And the door was shut, and a week later the storm burst.

But Noah was saved. His wife was saved. Shem, Ham and Japhet were saved. Their wives were saved. Fear and faith went hand in hand. But Noah's faith had saved his family. What peace that must have brought to his soul. Happy indeed is the godly parent who lives to see his children all safely in the Ark.

HE LOOKED FOR A CITY

HEBREWS 11:8-10

"By faith Abraham . . ." We begin with THE CALL. He was called "to go out into a place which he shoulder afterward receive for an inheritance." Abraham was a native of the city of Ur, on the west bank of the Euphrates. He seems to have been well-to-do. He was a descendant of Shem, Noah's youngest son, the one chosen by God to carry on the godly line. However, by the time Shem's descendants ran through eight or nine generations, the knowledge among them of the true and living God was just about lost. In all likelihood, Abraham was virtually a pagan, a worshipper of the moon. Until the Holy Spirit began to work in his soul.

For the time came when God revealed Himself to him. He gave him his call, a call destined to change him forever and also the history of the world. He was to leave his old way of life and step out by faith. He would be given a land of his own. He would become the father of many nations, and he would be blessed. Such was his call.

We think, too, of THE COST. The price of obedience was high. He was to get out of his father's house and turn his back upon his kindred. His first response was a hesitant kind of half obedience. He accompanied his father as far as Haran, a frontier town of the ancient Babylonian empire, devoted to the worship of the moon god; and there Abraham tarried. He made no further progress until his father died.

After the funeral he made his real move and set forth on his pilgrimage. Evidently he followed the ancient trade road across the Fertile Crescent until he came to Canaan. Then God spoke again: "Unto thy seed will I give this land," He said. The promise was repeated later on and greatly enlarged. The land grant to be his was to stretch from the Nile to the Euphrates, the hub of three continents and the most strategic spot on earth.

But now came THE CRISIS. Abraham discovered that the foul Canaanite was entrenched in the land, his land. Pagan though he once had been, Abraham must have been appalled by the filthiness and fierceness of Canaanite religion. How was he to get rid of the Canaanite? And, just as disconcerting, the land was in the grip of a famine. A crisis indeed! But God invariably puts us to the test at the commencement of a new venture of faith.

Then came THE CLIMAX. The Genesis account focuses on Canaan. The account in Hebrews 11 focuses on heaven. For that was Abraham's real goal: "He looked for a city which hath foundations, whose builder and maker is God." That great city drew him like a magnet. He was but a pilgrim and a stranger down here, the possession of the Promised Land of Canaan a mere incident in God's great plan. This Abraham understood. Beyond Canaan, his heart and true home were over there in Glory.

It should be thus with us. The Lord sets before us the vision of another country, a heavenly country. We start for that fair land the moment we are saved. Our true citizenship is up there so we are to be strangers and pilgrims down here. Our calling is to be ambassadors to those who live down here, and to urge them to join us over there.

BY FAITH SARAH

HEBREWS 11

Oh but she wanted a son! It was a common enough desire. Every devout woman in the Word, from Sarah to Elizabeth, longed for a son. It was a joyous occasion to be married. The birth of a girl was better than barrenness. But to give birth to a boy, to bring a man-child into the world! Why, that was the crown of joy for a Hebrew maid. For perhaps her son might turn out to be His Son, the long promised Seed of the woman, no less, the Savior of mankind.

So we come back to Sarah and HER LONGING. For Sarah had no son. Ishmael did not count though, once, she had imagined Abraham and Hagar could give her a surrogate son. The boy born of that union gave her nothing but grief. In the end, both Hagar and Ishmael had to be cast out. The whole thing had been a disaster.

So Sarah longed for a son. Above all else in this world, she wanted a son. She had everything else. Abraham was rich. He had flocks and herds and tents and camels and servants born in his house. And he was strong. The Canaanite tribes feared him. He was a mighty prince among them. But, for all his wealth and power, he could not buy Sarah a son. She was barren.

Which brings us to HER LAUGH. Abraham settled down at Hebron in the Promised Land. One day he was sitting in the door of his tent; and Sarah was within, inside the veil. Three mysterious visitors appeared walking his way, toward his tent. Abraham knew well enough who they were. One was God the Son. The other two were angels, Gabriel and Michael perhaps. They dined at Abraham's table. They paused. They had words for him before they went their way. Curiosity got the better of Sarah. She crept up to the partition to hear what was being said. "Nine months from now and Sarah will have a son," the spokesman said (Gen.18:10). Sarah burst out laughing. It was too funny for words! She was ninety, and Abraham was a hundred! No wonder Sarah laughed (17:17).

Then comes HER LIE. "Why did Sarah laugh?" God said. "Is there anything too hard for the Lord?" Frightened, Sarah lied. "I laughed not," she said. Imagine! Lying in the face of God Himself. And all God did was contradict her and correct her and leave it at that. Such is His grace. It is a good thing God does not mark and punish all our sins. If He did, He would soon depopulate the globe.

Which brings us to HER LOGIC. Hebrews 11 says, "She judged Him faithful Who had promised." She stopped laughing and doubting and became as great a believer as Abraham. She fixed her eyes on God. For the next nine months she looked for a son. Someone might say: "Maybe it will abort, you are so old." "NO!" She would say. "Maybe it will be a girl." "NO!" she would say. "Maybe you'll die, you are so old." "NO! Please stop making silly remarks," she would say, "or I'll start laughing again—for sheer joy. GOD has promised me a son, and a son I shall have. Indeed God has already named him—ISAAC ("Laughter") is his name."

Such was her logic. God had promised. What more could anyone want than that? So let us laugh at our doubts and at the difficulties in the way. God's promises are sure. They are backed by all the resources of His deity. What more, indeed, could we want than that?

BY FAITH RAHAB

HEBREWS 11:31

Rahab's faith was extraordinary. It not only saved her soul, it put her in the royal family and made her an ancestress of Christ. And she, a former Jericho harlot, is listed in the picture gallery of faith, along with such worthies as Enoch and Noah, Abraham, Isaac and Jacob, and David and Samuel. But her spiritual pilgrimage did not begin with faith, by any means, though she was eager enough to seize hold of salvation the moment the opportunity arose.

We are to think, first, of her FEAR. The Old Testament narrative tells of the coming of the two Hebrews to her house. She knew at once they were spies, but that only loosened her tongue. She was terrified. All Jericho was terrified. The walls of Jericho were great and strong, but walls are only as strong as those who defend them. And the people of Jericho were in mortal fear of the foe that had suddenly come marching up from the skyline and which now lay encamped nearby.

There was good reason for that fear. A generation ago this same people had overthrown and spoiled the land of Egypt. For some reason they had not invaded Canaan then, but everyone in Jericho expected them to invade Canaan now. The fear of the plagues of Egypt hung over Jericho. Rahab made no bones about it. It is not at all unusual for fear to come before faith. The work of conviction comes before the work of conversion.

We think next of her FALSEHOOD. She hid the two spies and shielded them from the King of Jericho's men. To do so, she had to tell a lie. The Holy Spirit records it but makes no comment. In actual fact, it is hard to see how she could have done anything else and still saved the spies, let alone her own life. In any case, it was a time of war; and a different ethic prevails in war. Killing, for instance, is countenanced in war when the occasion requires. So is deception. Moreover, the Holy Spirit makes no fuss about Rahab's falsehood. He chose to overlook it. It was this pagan woman's way of showing whose side she was on.

Then comes her FAITH. Before lowering the spies to safety, Rahab talked to them about her deepest need. No one had to tell her she was a sinner. What she needed was a Savior. She was in peril, and she knew it. The spies gave her a pledge. She was to tie a scarlet cord in her window. It would be the token of her faith. She wasted no time. The moment the messengers of God were gone, that scarlet cord was in place.

Her trust was in that token. It symbolized the blood of the covenant by which she was sealed. She was safe. That scarlet line told her so, all outward appearances to the contrary, notwithstanding. And the outward circumstances were ominous enough—the daily, eerie march of the somber Israelites, in utter silence, around doomed city. But Rahab's faith never failed. She knew Who she had believed and was persuaded that He was able to keep that which she'd committed unto Him against that day.

Finally, there was her FAMILY. Diligently she witnessed to them so that they too came and took shelter behind the scarlet cord. That was her old family. Not long after the fall of Jericho, and her so great salvation, she had a new family. The people of God became her people too. She took eagerly to that family. Indeed, one of the two spies, Salmon by name, married her. As a result, she became an ancestress of both David and a long line of kings and, above all, of Christ. Oh, for like precious faith!

THE GODS OF EGYPT
EXODUS 12:12

The Egyptian civilization was unrivaled in the ancient world. Its artifacts fill our museums and draw countless crowds who come to wonder and to stare. The Egyptians had eaten well of the tree of knowledge. Their brilliant minds were enlightened. We read of Moses that he was "learned in all wisdom of the Egyptians." His knowledge was co-extensive with that of the learned doctors at whose feet he sat. The Egyptians excelled in the arts and sciences. They had the technology and industry to build the pyramids. They were marvelous engineers. They were experts in agriculture, in navigation, in warfare and in astronomy. They built monuments which became wonders of the world and which have defied the tooth of time.

To this day we marvel at the pyramids. From a distance they look like mountains, rising sharply against the sky. Everything about them is big. Some two-and-a-half million blocks of limestone, weighing from two to five tons apiece (an aggregate of some 6 million tons), make up the mass of the Great Pyramid alone. When Moses and the enslaved Hebrews saw them, they were already at least a thousand years old. How did they build such things? We still do not know. We only know their brilliant minds were enlightened. Moses was called to wage a one-man war against this brilliant people.

Because there was another side to the Egyptians. Their foolish hearts were darkened. Professing themselves to be wise, they became fools and changed the glory of the incorruptible god into an image. Egypt was crowded with graven images, and their pantheon teemed with gods. There was HATHOR, the sky goddess, sometimes depicted as a cow. There was OSIRIS, who was married to his sister, ISIS. There was SET, the jealous and murderous brother of OSIRIS. There was THOTH, the moon god, the recorder of the deeds of the dead. There was the jackal-headed ANUBIS, the despoiler. And many more. It was against these gods of Egypt, led by Pharaoh himself, as the incarnation of RA, the sun gad, that Moses was sent. And it was these false and foolish gods Moses was to expose as empty, shattered and defeated, in his hand-to-hand combat with Pharaoh.

The gods of Egypt were <u>prevalent</u>. Every phase of Egyptian life was governed by the gods. They dominated life from the womb to the tomb. Moreover, they were <u>preposterous</u>, usually depicted as humans with the heads and features of animals and birds. There was the lion-headed SEKHMET, a goddess sent to punish people if they neglected the gods. There was HATHOR, the sky goddess, depicted as a cow. There was ANU-BIS, with the head of a jackal. There was THOTH, the moon god who kept the records which decided the doom of the dead. There was RA, the sun god of whom Pharaoh was the incarnation. There was no end to it, cats and crocodiles, bats and beetles. And the folly of it all lay in the fact that these gods were not only false, they were POWERLESS.

It was God's avowed intent, right from the start, to expose the utter impotence of these gods (Ex.12:12). Aaron's rod turned into a serpent and swallowed the rods of the magicians and poked fun at the serpent image Pharaoh wore as a crown on his brow. The Nile was worshipped as a source of life, so it was turned to blood. Frogs were worshipped as a symbol of fruitfulness, so God used them to plague the Egyptians. The pestilence on the cattle was aimed at the worship of animals. The plague of darkness showed RA, the sun god, to be powerless. And, of course, the last, terrible plague which brought death to every home, exposed the impotence of each and every Egyptian god.

So there Pharaoh sat, in all his pomp and splendor, with the resources of an empire at this command, powerless. And there stood Moses, the despised and detested shepherd, an abomination to the Egyptians, in his homespun, peasant's robes, clothed with power from on high. On the one hand, Egypt's ludicrous gods; on the other hand, Israel's living god. It is still that way. Forty years before, Moses had decided whose side he was on. Adopted into the Egyptian royal family, educated in Egypt's finest schools, pleasure and power and boundless prosperity all his to command, and offered the very throne itself, it would seem, Moses chose the living God, not this world's tin and tinsel gods. We must do the same.

THE PASSOVER

The <u>circumstances were dire enough</u>. The Hebrews were prisoners in Egypt, held in a Ghetto in Goshen. The king's command was still in force—wipe out the Jews. There could be no hope of escape, not so long as Pharaoh's soldiers guarded the Ghetto. As for the Promised Land, all hope of that was just about gone.

The Kinsman-Redeemer had come, but nothing had changed. Egypt had been leveled to the dust by plague after plague, but the Pharaoh was still on the throne. He remained unbroken, unbowed, unbelieving, determined <u>not</u> to let his captive Hebrews go. Such were the circumstances. They were dire enough.

<u>And the solution was drastic enough</u>. God's avenging angel would smite all the firstborn of Egypt. God would give them a holocaust. It would put such fear of God in Pharaoh's heart that, out of sheer terror, he would finally let the Hebrew captives go. The avenging angel of death would be sent forth by God to smite and kill every firstborn of man and beast throughout the length and breadth of the land.

But what about the Hebrews? Hebrew homes were in Goshen; and Goshen was part of Egypt, and all Egypt was under the interdict of God. Something would have to be done. But what? God gave His people a conditional guarantee from death.

<u>The guarantee was distinct enough</u>. A lamb must be taken, a lamb without blemish or spot. It must be slain. Its blood must be applied to the lintels and doorposts of each individual home. The avenging angel would <u>pass over</u> every house so marked, and the blood of the slain lambs would speak for the people of God. So the Hebrews remained in their blood-sealed homes, feasted on their Passover lambs and made ready for the march.

Now let us look at Moses. He brought the message: "When I see the blood I will pass over you." A great deal of truth was intertwined with the death of the Passover Lamb. From a lamb it became the Lamb (pointing directly to Christ) and finally your lamb, injecting the personal note. A house could be too little for a lamb, but the Lamb was never too little for the house.

Then, too, the Passover was a milestone. With Abel, it was a lamb for the individual. With Abraham, a lamb for the family. Now it is a lamb for the nation. At Calvary, it would be a lamb for the world. So Moses brought the message: "When I see the blood." The avenging angel, however, would not be deterred by a bucket of blood on the doorstep. It had to be applied. Paint on the doorposts would not do. There was no cheap way to secure redemption. A sign, "Moses lives here," (for instance), nailed to the door, would not do. Moses was a younger son, so he was safe. But he had an elder brother, Aaron. Aaron wasn't safe. And Moses had an eldest son, Gersham. He was in peril until the blood was applied. Once the blood had been applied, however, all was well. At peace with God, and sheltered by the blood Moses could feast and face the triumphant future God had planned.

To some, perhaps, even in Israel, the message of an avenging angel, and salvation by blood, must have seemed nonsense, repulsive even, the message of a madman. If there were such skeptics in the camp that night, and if they followed the dictates of their human reason, scorning Divine revelation, they found out too late their mistake.

There was the message. It was followed by the miracle. Who but God could have known, in each and every house, who the firstborns were, or have selected, in every barn and field, the firstborn of every cow or sheep or dog or cat? It was uncanny. It was unerring. It was God. And all of it, pointing with steady finger down the unborn ages to Jesus, the true Passover Lamb, Who paid for our redemption with His blood.

When God Makes A Move

It was time for a change. It might have seemed to some to be long overdue. Not so! God moves according to His own timetable. He had long since told Abraham that his seed would be in a foreign land for 400 years. The date for the change had been marked on God's calendar all the time. Now the time had come. The children of Israel, enslaved in Egyptian bondage, were to be redeemed, removed and resettled. It is instructive to observe four spiritual laws which seem to come into effect at such times.

First, there were CHANGING TIMES. The Israeli presence in Goshen had long troubled the Egyptians in a general sort of a way. They were different. They belonged to a different God. What if they should side one day with one of Egypt's foes? Then there arose that king "who knew not Joseph." And all of a sudden everything was changed. The comfortable state of compromise was over. It was the first step in a movement which would change the world.

Now came CHURNING TIDES. The Israelites awoke one morning to the din of war. Pharaoh's army had marched into Goshen. Behind them came the barbed wire, the guard dogs trained to kill, the chains, the taskmasters and all the paraphernalia of oppression. And a new, terrible law: "Cast all newborn males into the Nile." Churning tides, indeed. The people of God had become too comfortable in this present evil world. They must be made to see it as God sees it, the sworn enemy of God and all things holy. Oppression and more oppression for now the world's mask was off, and its hideous, hate-marked face revealed. It is God's way.

What churning tides were unleashed in 1939, for instance, when the German army stormed into Poland. The turmoil went on and on until the whole world was engulfed. Millions of men were uprooted from their homes and sent to distant lands. Out of it came a new generation of men and women, who had traveled to those lands and who went back as missionaries. The churning tides prepared the way. The modern missionary era began.

Next came CHEERLESS TOILS. In Egypt the people of God were put to a new kind of work. They made bricks for Pharaoh. Pharaoh had vast plans. He wanted treasure cities built. He wanted bricks. The hated Hebrews were whipped into line. They must make his bricks. More and more bricks. He urged on his slave drivers, and they goaded the unhappy Hebrews. "Was this," they must have wondered, "was this the way to the Promised Land?" It seemed like a cynical joke.

And then the unexpected and unexplained took place. The people began to multiply. The more pressure the world applied, the more the people of God multiplied. It was the same in the Book of Acts with the infant Church. The pressure of persecution went on for about three hundred years until there were more Christians than pagans in Rome. Yes! God was still on the throne!

Finally we see certain CHOSEN TOOLS. There was Jochabed and Amram who dared to have a son in such troubled and terrible times. There was Moses, the child born to become a kinsman-redeemer to Israel in the fulness of time. There was Miriam, the brave sister of Moses who watched over the infant in his ark of rushes in the Nile, fearless of Egyptian soldiers and Nile crocodiles alike. Others followed. There was Aaron sent to be a companion to Moses and High Priest to Israel. And Joshua, chosen of Moses to succeed him and to take possession, at last, of the long-promised land. Thus, though in the onward march of time He buries His workers, He still carries on His work. We'll understand it better bye and bye.

MOSES AT HOREB
EXODUS 3:1;17:6;33:6

Horeb is mentioned three times in Exodus in connection with Moses. Horeb and Sinai are closely linked. Horeb was the mountain range, Sinai was one of its peaks. It was at Horeb Moses met God.

The first time it was at the burning bush. God showed HIS GOVERN-MENT, His absolute sovereignty over human affairs. Moses came, with his father-in-law's flocks, to what the Holy Spirit describes as "the backside of the desert." It is also called "the Mountain of God." That is significant. When a person is in the will of God, everything about him bears the mark of God— a man becomes "a man of God," a rod becomes "the rod of God," a word becomes "the word of God," a mountain becomes "the mountain of God."

So Moses came to Horeb and to the burning bush. He was drawn aside to see this most unusual of usual sights—a bush ablaze with fierce flames and wrapped in fire. Yet, despite the devouring fire the bush was not consumed. Moses was arrested. However God had to get beyond the eye of Moses to his ear, for "faith cometh by hearing" the Bible says

(Rom.10:17). "Moses! Moses! Remove your shoes," God said. "And Moses hid his face," the Holy Spirit adds.

A thorn bush in the fire but not consumed. That thorn bush was Israel. The fire, the growing oppression of the Pharaoh. Yet, for all his power, Pharaoh could not make an end of God's people. And who was this Pharaoh? A speck of dust, inflated with pride, surrounded by meaningless pomp, worshipping cats and cows and crocodiles and creeping things.

God began with Moses' feet. He told him to remove the shoes from off his feet. That is where He usually begins. Our feet have to do with our standing. When the stone came hurtling out of eternity to smash Nebuchadnezzar's golden image, it did not strike the head. It smote the feet. So, at Horeb, there was a lesson in GOVERNMENT. True, the bush was ablaze; but God was in the bush, and that changed everything. Pharaoh was up against God.

The second time Horeb is mentioned, Moses gets a lesson in GRACE. At the beginning of any new venture, God allows us to be tested. Thus Israel came to Rephidim and the shadow of a great fear. For there was no water, no water at all, not even bitter water as at Marah. Cattle lowed in anguish. Children cried to their parents. The people turned on Moses and threatened to kill him. Moses turned to God: "They be almost ready to stone me," he cried. "Take your rod," God commanded. It was a rod of judgment. With that rod he had turned the rivers of Egypt to blood. It was poised to fall on this rebellious people. Instead, it fell on the Rock—and the water of life poured forth. It was a lesson in grace, the Rock being a type of Christ.

The third time Horeb is mentioned, Moses gets a lesson in GLORY. He had summoned by God back up the Mount, and he had been gone a long time, or so it seemed, to rebellious Israel. Apostasy took over. Aaron made a golden calf, and the people abandoned themselves to lustful singing and lewd dancing. Then Moses returned, and judgment followed. In despair Moses threw himself into he arms of God. "Show me Thy way," he said and then, more daring still, "show me Thy glory." And so God hid this troubled servant in the cleft of the Rock, for only in such a secure hiding place could he be safe when God's effulgent glory was revealed. God showed Moses His goodness and His grace—for that is His glory, as we shall know at last in Glory itself.

ANGEL'S FOOD

PSALM 78:24-25

It never occurs to us that angels eat! Still less, that God would take royal daintees from their bountiful board on high and pour them out to mortal men in hunger in a waste howling wilderness on a remote island planet in space called Earth. Yet this is what happened. God gave them "the corn of heaven." He gave them "angels' food." And that wondrous "bread from heaven" not only satisfied their hunger, it was also a type of Jesus Himself, the Bread of God upon Whom we feed as we wend our way through the wilderness of this world to the Promised Land above.

The story of the manna, as it was called, begins with THE DISCONTENT OF THE PEOPLE. They were a people recently redeemed from the house of bondage and from the sentence of death. They had been redeemed by power, put under the blood, baptized unto Moses in the sea, gathered to the living God and were moving homewards. But they were hungry, and the wilderness had nothing to offer; just as the world has nothing to offer our hungry souls. So the people murmured and complained. They thought nostalgically of how well they were fed on onions, leeks and garlic in Egypt. They conveniently forget the toil, the sweat, and the tears, the lash and the scourge and the genicidal law which destined their young to sure and certain death. Instead they murmured against Moses and against God.

Then came THE DISCOVERY OF THE PEOPLE. They awoke one morning to a world turned white as though with frost. But it was nothing of the kind. God had spread a table for them in the wilderness. They called the mysterious food "manna." It was all about them, well within the reach of all, of easy access to young and old, bread from heaven, sweet to the taste, satisfying to their needs. It could be baked or boiled. The rabbis had a tradition that it tasted of whatever kind of food a man desired. It would melt in the mouth.

Thus God meets our spiritual hunger. He showers upon us all that there is in Christ and in His Word to satisfy our hungry souls.

Take the Word of God, for instance. We need only reach out our hands and take it, 773, 692 Divinely inspired words (592, 439 in the Old Testament and 181, 253 in the New), and each and every word God breathed. What an inexhaustible provision for our daily spiritual needs. Christ too! He is the true Bread from heaven, manna enough and to spare for our hungry souls.

But then came THE DISOBEDIENCE OF THE PEOPLE. The rules for gathering the manna were simple and they were intended as a test of obedience. There were three rules. First there was the simple rule. The manna came down with the dew and vanished with the sun. The person too lazy to gather his daily supply went hungry. There was nothing else.

Nor could it be stored. A person could not gather enough on Monday to last all week. It perished if an attempt was made to hoard it. Similarly, we must feast on the Word day by day. And we must be up before the sun waxes hot, that is, before the rush and bustle of our busy lives rob us of our time for gathering our daily bread.

There was also the Sabbath rule. No manna came on the Sabbath, God's day of rest; but a double portion came the day before, and stayed fresh. The principle of rest is essential to life. Even planets have periods of growth and periods of rest.

Finally there was the special rule. A pot of manna was miraculously preserved in the tabernacle, generation after generation, to remind us that God will feed us until we want no more.

MICHAEL THE ARCHANGEL

JUDE 9

The heavenly host have their hierarchies. There are angels and archangels, there are principalities and powers (owing allegiance to Satan), there are thrones and dominions (who render homage and service to God), there are the rulers of this world's darkness, there wicked spirits in high places, and there are the cherubim and the seraphim. Michael is an archangel. Just before the voice of divine inspiration and supernatural revelation falls silent, Jude gives us an unexpected look at one page in Michael's history. It has to do with the burial of Moses.

First, there was THE CONFRONTATION. It appears that when Moses was buried, in a remote and hidden spot on Mount Nebo, Satan suddenly turned up at the funeral. No doubt Michael recognized the enemy at once. He was the author of sin, the Father of lies, the old serpent, the deceiver, the old lion, the destroyer, the angel of light, the deluder of mankind. Michael knew him of old. He had know him when he was the anointed cherub, the choirmaster of heaven, glorious in beauty, awesome in power. He knew him now as ruler of an empire of fallen angels, demons and men.

Michael is known as the archangel, the only angelic being so called. He is Israel's patron and the prince who stands on their side in the unseen world. He is Gabriel's ally in the defense of the nation of Israel from its human and satanic foes. In a coming day, Michael will throw Satan from the skies (Rev.12). So Satan showed up at the funeral of Moses, confronted Michael and demanded that Moses' body be turned over to him.

Now comes THE CONTENTION. In Hebrew history Moses ranks with Abraham, founder of the Hebrew racial family, and with David, founder of the Hebrew royal family. It was Moses who gave the Hebrew nation its magnificent legal code. It was Moses who had emancipated the Hebrews from slavery and saved them from extinction. It was Moses who organized them into a great nation. It was Moses who gave them their vibrant and Divinely ordained religion. It was Moses who brought the Hebrew people right up to the border of the Promised Land. He is mentioned by name at least seven hundred times in the Bible.

No sooner was Moses dead than the Israelites were ready to deify him, and Satan was eager to oblige. That was why he turned up on Mount Nebo, armed with enormous power. He wanted the body of Moses to be handed to him so that he would make it the center of a rival idolatrous Hebrew reli-gion. Michael was no match for Lucifer, fallen though he was, so he wisely stood aside. "The Lord rebuke you," he said. That left Lucifer face to face with God. And Lucifer is no match for Him.

Moreover, God wanted that body, for resurrection. Satan backed down; and the body was buried and its graveside hidden from men but protected by God.

Then suddenly the body of Moses turned up, on a mountain in the Promised Land during the days of Jesus. It had been raised from the dead, and Moses had come back to visit the incarnate God on the Mount of

Transfiguration. Banned from the Promised Land by God for losing his temper, for speaking unadvisedly with his lips and for smiting the Rock, a disappointed Moses had climbed Mount Nebo to at least <u>see</u> the Promised Land. Now God lifted the ban; and Moses, in person, in his body, appeared on the holy mount. What a triumph for Moses! God had kept the old warrior's body hidden away where even Satan himself could not find it.

So Gabriel won after all. And so did Moses. And so did God!

The Ashes And The Fire

The first seven chapters of Leviticus are concerned with the various offerings the Hebrew people were to bring to God. The details were given meticulously, and more and more requirements were added. We tend to read these chapters with varying degrees of bewilderment and impatience. For all these ritual requirements belong to the long, long ago. Why should we be concerned with them now? They are obsolete. Calvary and Pentecost have swept them away. Besides, the meaning of all these things escapes us. Even the Jews themselves would be hard put to it to interpret the true meaning of all these rituals and rules.

Maybe so. But they are evidently of great interest to God. He inspired the writing down of all these details. These verses are as much "God-breathed" as our favorite New Testament texts. Indeed, God was not content with writing it all down once—burnt offering, meal offering, peace offering, sin offering, trespass offering. When He had finished He went back over the same ground, adding fresh details in the form of sundry "laws"—the <u>law</u> of the burnt offering, the <u>law</u> of the sin offering and so on. He delights in every detail for, one and all, the offerings speak of Christ, in His flawless life and in His atoning death.

The <u>law</u> of the burnt offering was concerned with two added details, with the fire and with the ashes. <u>The fire</u> was to never go out. That reminds us that God's wrath against sin is as fierce today as it was when it kindled the lake of fire. The crime of Calvary has heated it seven times hotter than before. It will never go out. That is a terrible truth, but it is consistent with the holiness of God.

The <u>law</u> of the burnt offering was concerned also with <u>the ashes</u>. They were infinitely precious to God. After the fire had burned all night, consuming the burnt offering, the priest approached the brazen altar in fine linen. Reverently he collected the ashes and carried them outside the camp to a clean place.

The ashes remind us of a great truth. We can stir a smoldering fire and get sparks and blow upon the embers and bring back the fire and, with fresh fuel, again have roaring flames. But we can stir ashes forever and get nothing. There is nothing left to burn. This tells us that it is impossible to stir God's wrath against the believer. The sacrificial work of Christ is so complete, His substitutionary work so effective, that nothing can ever rekindle God's wrath so far as we are concerned. That is consistent with the love of God. Neither His <u>eternal</u> wrath nor His <u>end-time</u> wrath can fall upon us. He has <u>not</u> appointed <u>us</u> to wrath but to obtain salvation (1 Thess. 5:9).

Years ago a fire was sweeping across the prairie, driven by the wind. A man and his family stood in its path. The man kindled a fire at this feet. It took hold and, driven by the wind, burned out a swath of the grass. "Come and stand where the fire has been," the man said. The family did so, and the approaching holocaust passed them by. There was nothing left there to burn.

That is where the believer stands—where the fire has been. His salvation is assured.

THE HOLY OINTMENT (1)
EXODUS 30:22-33

There was nothing like it in this world. It was prepared from a special formula revealed to Moses by divine inspiration of the Holy Ghost. We are told HOW IT WAS PRODUCED—five hundred shekels of this, two hundred and fifty shekels of that, a little of this and some of that, no more, no less. The ingredients, spices drawn from here and there, were rare and costly and were mixed with a lavish hand.

The shekel used for weighing these costly spices, worth a king's ransom, was the shekel of the sanctuary. Among the Jews the ephah was used for dry measure, the cubit was used for lineal measure, the hin was used for liquid measure and the shekel was used for measuring weight.

The shekel of the sanctuary, the sacred shekel, was heavier than the ordinary shekel. God expects more from us, when he weighs us, than we expect of ourselves. In ourselves we are all like poor, lost Belshazzar—weighed in the balances and found wanting. We can persuade ourselves that we have performed in a satisfactory way, but our scales are inaccurate. So much of our performance is made up of personal ambition, pride, love of position, love of praise and such like things. God sifts all that out when He weighs us.

It was by the high and unerring standard, the shekel of the sanctuary, that God weighed Christ. "I am well pleased," He said (Matt.3:17). We can be sure God used no light-weight measure in passing verdict on Him.

Five hundred shekels. Think of it! Half a shekel was the ransom price for an Israelite under the Law (Lev.30:11-16). When numbered, each man had to bring half a silver shekel—the price of his redemption. A full shekel tells us that the ransom has not only been paid, but fully and adequately paid. Five hundred shekels implies a measure of redemption only God can comprehend. Five hundred plus two hundred and fifty plus two hundred and fifty plus another five hundred tells of a redemption beyond all human thought.

We are told WHY IT WAS PROVIDED: "And thou shalt anoint the tabernacle.. and the ark, and the table, and the candlestick, and the altar of incense, and the altar of burnt offering, and the laver." In the outer court—where grace was shown, in the holy place where God was served, in the Holiest of all, where glory was seen, all was made fragrant by the anointing. God wants the fragrance of Christ to be everywhere—everywhere! Aaron and his sons were to be anointed and also prophets and kings. All who serve the Lord must carry with them the fragrance of Christ Whose very name "is as ointment poured forth" (Song of Sol.1:3).

Finally, we are told HOW IT WAS PROTECTED. It was not to be copied. "Who so compoundeth any like it, or whosoever putteth any of it upon a stranger shall even be cut off from his people." Christ did not come so that we might imitate Him, but so that we may be indwelt by Him. He Who gave His life for us now gives His life to us so that everywhere we go we might carry with us His fragrance. May we do just that!.

THE HOLY OINTMENT (2)
EXODUS 30:22-33

It was unique. The Jews were forbidden to make its like. It was to be neither imitated or profaned. Its ingredients and their amounts are given. It all speaks of Christ. First, we have the myrrh. It points to the passion of Christ. Myrrh was a resinous gum derived from a tree of the terebinth family. It grows in the dry desert wastes of Arabia. The myrrh, used in making the anointing oil, is described as "pure" myrrh. The Hebrew word for "pure" is said to describe the swallow, darting in the sky. The Lord Jesus, in His life, was as free as the birds of the air. Christ's death was voluntary. His death was like the free-flowing myrrh. Myrrh was obtained by incisions made in the tree. It was used at weddings and funerals. It added fragrance in life's gladdest and saddest hours. Five hundred shekels by weight was the contribution of the myrrh to the anointing oil. That amounted to one third of the total weight of the whole. The same is true of the four gospels also. The heavy emphasis, in all of them, is the death of Christ. John's gospel, for instance, devotes about half of its space to the events of the last week of our Lord, to the events, that is, connected with His death.

The next two ingredients were sweet cinnamon and sweet calamus. They point to the person of Christ. It took two ingredients to depict the Person of Christ because Christ united two natures in His Being, the human and divine. He was both God and man. Cinnamon comes from an evergreen tree of the laurel family. The inner bark yields a light brown spice. In olden times it was more valuable than gold. The Lord in His Person was like that—an evergreen! He was the "blessed Man" of the first psalm. "His leaf also shall not wither," the psalmist said. He was the God-man of Philippians 2:5, His whole life His Deity. Death itself could not overcome Him. When the time cane He lay down His life Himself. He dismissed His Spirit Himself.

The calamus was a reed, pointing to the sky, a species of tall grass—depicting the fragrant humanity of Christ. He grew up as a tender plant, rooted to earth but pointing to the sky. The plant had to be crushed before its full fragrance could be obtained. The holy anointing oil called for two hundred and fifty shekels of cinnamon and the same amount of calamus. The deity and humanity were perfectly balanced in the Person of Christ.

The <u>cassia</u> points to the <u>perfection</u> of Christ. It belonged to the same family as the cinnamon. A full five hundred shekel measure of cassia was required. The cassia reminds us of the Lord Jesus as He is presented in the typology of the Lord Jesus. The prophetic 45th Psalm said of Him: "All thy garments smell of cassia" (Ps.45:8). This plant grows where others die. It was used to blend all the other ingredients of the holy ointment. Oh, the pungency of the holiness and perfection of Christ. Bullying Pilate himself was overwhelmed by it. It threw wicked Herod into sharp reaction and open ridicule. It was strong enough to conquer the grave.

But the ointment, with all its pungent ingredients, needed one more thing—<u>oil</u>. The oil points to the <u>position</u> of Christ as the Anointed One. The oil speaks of the Holy Spirit. The oil which tool all these various fragrant excellences of the Lord Jesus (symbolized by the myrrh, the cinnamon, the calamus and the cassia) and blended them together. It was the Holy Spirit Who took the various excellences of Christ—His passion, His Person (both human and divine), His perfection—and transformed them from a collection of superlatives into one glorious, breath-taking whole and blended them into one inimitable fragrance.

One of the Lord's most eloquent titles was "the Christ," the Anointed One. He is God's anointed priest. He ministers thus in heaven, filling all that glorious place with the pervading fragrance of His presence. He is God's anointed prophet. Truly, no man spake like this man. And He is God's anointed King, coming soon to restore Edenic conditions to this world.

In the meantime, He anoints His own. Nobody was allowed to imitate that ointment, but God was willing to <u>share</u> it with us. Nobody can imitate the life of Christ. But we may have His fragrance shed abroad in our hearts by the Holy Spirit.

THE INCENSE
EXODUS 30:34-38

The incense was burned on the golden altar in the Holy Place of the Temple. On the day of atonement it was carried in a golden censer into the immediate presence of God in the Holy of Holies just beyond the Temple veil It had four ingredients. They were blended together in the order in which they are listed—stacte, onycha, galbanum and frankincense. Incense is a symbol of prayer, ascending to God in a fragrant could from the golden altar. It is hard for us to pray so the Holy Spirit helps us and makes intercession for us (Rom.8:26-27). His instructions regarding the incense are a step in this direction.

The stacte suggests PATIENCE in prayer. The Greek word "stacte" translates a Hebrew word which literally means "to drop" or "to distill." The thought seems to be "to distill as the dew." Dew is distilled secretly, in stillness, and in silence. It takes time for dew to form. That is the first ingredient of prayer—patience. We must take time to pray. We must be still.

The onycha suggests PENITENCE in prayer. The Hebrew word is thought to refer to a perfumed mollusk which had to be crushed to yield its fragrance. This suggests to us that we should be crushed by the enormity of our sins. We might well be overwhelmed by our sins, by their constant repetition and by their continuing reign. Repentance is what we need, penitence in prayer.

The galbanum suggests PRAISE in prayer. The word comes from a root meaning "to be fat, or fertile," possibly referring to the sap—the life, strength and virility of the tree, the pith and heart of the plant. Galbanum added strength and vitality to the other ingredients of the holy incense. It is the rising sap which brings out the leaves and the flower and the fruit of the plant. It is praise which brings life into our prayers. Praise is the most important part of prayer, closely skin to worship.

The frankincense suggests PETITION in prayer. Frankincense is mentioned repeatedly in the Bible. It was one of the things the wise men brought to the infant Jesus. The word comes from a root meaning "to be white." It comes from the same root as the word "Lebanon"—"the white mountain," referring to the snow that crowns the mountain's brow. If there is one thing which must mark our petitions, it is purity. God says if we regard iniquity in our hearts, the Lord will not hear us (Ps.66:18). We ask and receive not because we ask amiss to consume it on our lusts.

The gum from which frankincense was derived comes from a plant in which the number five predominates. It bears five petals and ten stamens. The fruit is five-sided, and there are five species of the plant. In Scripture the number five is associated with grace. The frankincense reminds us our prayer ascends to just such a throne, a throne of grace (Heb.4:16). Incidentally, frankincense comes from a tree which grows on bare inhospitable rock. This reminds us that prayer draws its strength from Christ, the Rock of Ages.

There was one other ingredient to the incense—salt. Salt suggests PUNGENCY in prayer. How dull prayer meetings often become! If our speech is to be seasoned with salt (Col.4:6), how much more our prayers! Surely we should give as much attention to making our prayers interesting as we do to making our conversation interesting. It is bad enough to be a bore in general speech. It is well nigh criminal to bore people with our uninspired, insipid, repetitious prayers. Surely it is time we came with the disciples to the Lord Jesus and say to Him—"Lord, teach us to pray."

THE FEASTS: PASSOVER, UNLEAVENED BREAD AND FIRSTFRUITS
LEVITICUS 23

The Old Testament called for the annual celebration of seven mandatory and meaningful feasts. These feasts were separated into two groups. Four of them took place at the commencement of the religious year. Then came a pause, after which the three remaining feasts were kept. These feasts are prophetic in character. The first four feasts anticipated Christ's first coming; the last three anticipated Christ's second coming. The 2000-year period covered by the Church Age separates between the two.

We shall begin with THE COMMENCEMENT FEASTS, the first four feasts which were fulfilled at Christ's first coming. Three of these anticipate the work of the <u>Savior</u>. The remaining one anticipates the work of the <u>Spirit</u>.

The feast of <u>Passover</u> points to our <u>redemption</u>. On the tenth day of the month the people took a lamb, free from all blemish and kept it tethered until the fourteenth day. During this period it was closely watched. It was killed on the fourteenth day "between the two evenings" (between the sixth hour and the ninth hour). On the original Passover, the night of the Exodus its blood was applied so that those sheltering behind it would be saved from the avenging angel's sword.

The feast of <u>unleavened bread</u> (which lasted a week) was closely associated with Passover. The Passover lamb was killed on the fourteenth day. Immediately afterwards, on the fifteenth day, a week-long feast, known as the feast of unleavened bread, took place. The Hebrews were to thoroughly cleanse their houses of all leaven. Leaven in Scripture is used by the Holy Spirit as a type of sin. The feast of unleavened bread points to our <u>regeneration</u>. The old is purged out, the new takes it place.

Two of the feasts lasted a week, the others were one-day affairs. The feasts that occupy a single day point to some specific act of God— Passover, for example, takes us straight to Calvary. Feasts that lasted seven or eight days (unleavened bread and tabernacles) point to future events destined to span well-defined periods of time, namely the Church Age and the Millennial Age.

Note God's order with the feast of unleavened bread. First the blood was applied. Then came feasting on the lamb. Only then was leaven put out of the house. That is God's order. First there has to be redemption. Then a clean lifestyle must follow. God's house is prepared as God's home. The Hebrew housewife was diligent in her search for lurking leaven. She scoured every cupboard, every nook and cranny of the house to make sure that not so much as a scrap of leaven remained.

In the New Testament leaven is a picture of hidden sin. Leaven in a loaf of bread, for instance speaks of those things which, once introduced, continue to work away in secret until their activity is killed by fire. Throughout the whole period of seven days, vigilance had to be maintained lest leaven be somehow introduced. During this Church Age in which we live constant watch must be maintained that no corrupting influence lurks in our homes and that hidden sin is not allowed to remain unjudged in our hearts.

The feast of <u>firstfruits</u> points to our <u>resurrection</u>. This feast was kept on the first day of the week, on the Sunday after Passover. This was the very day Christ arose from the dead. The farmer cut one golden sheaf from the harvest field and waved it before the Lord and over the whole field. It foreshadowed the full harvest soon to come. The feast of firstfruits was fulfilled when the Lord was raised from the dead and when many other dead people arose at the same time, went into Jerusalem, and appeared unto many (Matt.27:52-53). These people correspond to the wave sheaf. In <u>His</u> resurrection and in <u>their</u> resurrection, we see the sure promise and guarantee of <u>our</u> resurrection. All these things the Savior accomplished for us at His first coming. He has <u>saved</u> us, <u>sanctified</u> us and <u>secured</u> us. We can rest assured as to that.

THE FEASTS: PENTECOST
LEVITICUS 23

The seven Old Testament feasts were divided into two sections. The first four commenced the series, and had reference to events connected with the first coming of Christ. Of these three, direct our attention to the work of the Savior. The fourth, <u>the feast of Pentecost</u>, directs our attention to the work of <u>the Spirit</u>.

The word "Pentecost" comes to us from the Greek. It is the Greek word for fifty. Because it was fifty days from the feast of firstfruits to Pentecost, this feast is sometimes called "the feast of weeks." There were seven full weeks to which was added another day. Thus the feast of firstfruits and the feast of Pentecost were celebrated on the first day of the week. These Old Testament feasts anticipated the end of the Jewish Sabbath and a new emphasis on the first day of the week as a day of rest and rejoicing.

"When the day of Pentecost was fully come," says Luke in recording the momentous events in the upper room (Acts 2:1). The feast had come and gone for some fifteen hundred years, now it had fully come. As all the

170

typology connected with it was fulfilled, the Old Testament shadows gave way to the New Testament substance. The Holy Spirit came in a new and living way. Judaism was replaced by the Church. The annual ritual, with its burnt offerings, with its sin offering and peace offering and with its two loaves, was swept aside. A new day had dawned.

On the day of Pentecost a hundred and twenty individual believers in Christ assembled in the upper room, a room full of memories for the disciples. The Church was born in that room with the sound of a mighty, rushing wind, and amid a blaze of cloven tongues of fire. In that upper room the Holy Spirit baptized a hundred and twenty separate believers into one body, "one loaf." As the wind drives away the chaff, so that mighty, rushing Pentecostal wind swept away the past which was centered in a now dead Judaism. The cloven tongues of fire symbolized the new cleansing and irresistible power now inherent in the Church, the mystical body of Christ. The loaf represents the one body, in contrast with the multiple grains of corn on the wave sheaf. Over a hundred individual believers went into the upper room. One body, one church came out.

The Old Testament ritual, however, actually called for two loaves, not just one. That was because Pentecost took place in two stages. Only Jews were present in the upper room on the actual day of Pentecost. Later on, in the house of the Roman centurion, Cornelius, Gentiles were added to the Church. The same apostle was the chosen agent of the Holy Spirit on both occasions. The same phenomena of tongues was present both times—the first time to convince the mass of unbelieving Jews in Jerusalem, the second time to convince the skeptical Jewish members of the Church. There were two loaves—but there was only "one bread and one body (1 Cor.10:17). Gentiles did not have to become Jews in order to become Christians. Jews and Gentiles were impartially baptized by the Spirit into the same mystical body of Christ. The middle wall of partition between Jews and Gentiles was swept away (Eph.4:4-6;2:13-16).

Before long, Gentiles would become a permanent and overwhelming majority in the Church. Note that there was leaven in the two loaves. This was because the loaves represent the Church which has never been wholly free from sin.

The process, begun at Pentecost, goes on, for the Holy Spirit continues to add new members to the mystical body of Christ. Thankfully it will be when Christ comes again (Eph.5:25-27).

THE FEASTS: TRUMPETS, ATONEMENT, TABERNACLES

The first four feasts all pointed to the first coming of the Lord Jesus. They had to do with the <u>commencement</u> of God's personal invasion of <u>history</u>, to the <u>work of the Savior</u>, in terms of redemption, regeneration and resurrection, and also to the work of the Spirit.

Then came a pause of length. The feasts of the commencement period were counted by <u>days</u>. The Passover was killed on the fourteenth day. Unleavened bread began the next day. On the morrow after the next Sabbath, firstfruits was celebrated. Fifty days were counted from then to Pentecost, and to the <u>work of the Spirit</u>.

But there was no counting of days to the next feast (trumpets). We are simply told it fell on the seventh month. For <u>this</u> time lapse foreshadowed the time from Pentecost to the Rapture of the Church. We know the approximate time covered by this period, but the actual date of that event is unknown. More particularly the feast of trumpets looked ahead to future events connected with the Nation of Israel.

Thus we come to <u>THE COMPLETION FEASTS</u>, trumpets, atonement and tabernacles. Just as the first four feasts all anticipated the first coming of Christ, so the last three feasts all look ahead to the second coming of Christ. Just as the first four feasts were all fulfilled to the letter, and to the day, at the Lord's first coming, so the last three feasts will also be fulfilled to the letter and to the day. We can be sure of that.

The feast of <u>Trumpets</u> focuses on the Gathering. Trumpets figured prominently in Israel's national life. Two silver trumpets were made from the redemption money given by the Hebrews for the building of the tabernacle. They were sounded when the tribes were called upon to march, when it was necessary to sound an alarm because danger threatened, and when all the assembly was required to appear before the Lord. The prophet

Isaiah tells how "the great trumpet" will regather the scattered Jewish people in the end times (27:13). The first beginnings of this return has already begun. Already Jews back in the Promised Land number several million. During the Period covered by the Apocalypse trumpets will herald some of its events—in particular seven trumpets will sound as the Antichrist comes and furthers his nefarious plans (Rev.8-9).

The feast of <u>atonement</u> focuses on the Grief. In reality this feast was a fast, a time of national conviction and repentance. It was the day when the sins of the nation were covered up for another year. It anticipates the day when the Jewish remnant, in the end times, will see the returning Christ and will be convicted because of their age-long rejection of Him.

The feast of <u>tabernacles</u> focuses on the Glory. It was celebrated after the harvest was gathered in (Deut.6:13). It was a week-long festival of praise and joy. It anticipated the millennial reign of Christ. An extra day (an eighth day) was added. In Scripture the number eight is associated with resurrection and a new beginning. The music scale illustrates this. There are eight notes in the scale but the eighth note is the same as the first one, only it is an octave higher.

The millennium will end in judgment; but that will not be the final end, for God will begin again, but on a higher note. He will create a new heaven and a new earth and usher in an endless, eternal day of bliss and joy.

These things told in Old Testament typology in the annual Jewish feasts will as surely come to pass as did the things which pertained to the Lord's first coming. Any day now, the trumpet will sound. The Church will be gone, and Israel will enter into its own.